HAUNTING YEARS

HAUNTING YEARS

*The Commentaries of a
War Territorial*

by

WILLIAM LINTON ANDREWS

HUTCHINSON & CO. (Publishers) LTD.
34-36 Paternoster Row, LONDON, E.C.4

A FOREWORD

WE FORGET BECAUSE WE MUST

I CALL them haunting years, for nothing in our time will haunt us like the War. Our dead comrades live on in our thoughts, appealingly, as if afraid to be forgotten. Peace came, but not at once for those who survived. The War pressed down on some of us like a doom for years after the last shot was fired.

I was luckier than most, but three years as an infantryman in France had worn me down. For some years after the War, like many, many others who had been there a long time, I woke almost every night in terror from a nightmare of suffocation by gas, or of being trapped by a bombardment from which I ran this way and that, or of fighting a bayonet duel with a gigantic Prussian Guardsman.

The specialists told me the best thing I could do was to forget the War and build up with hearty feeding—porridge, apples with their skins, potatoes with their jackets, oatmeal cakes, wholemeal bread.

The advice on diet jumped with my humour. I craved for things rich and greasy and feeding. When I was coming home from the trenches on leave it was always sausages and eggs and tomatoes fried together that I longed for most. And one of the happiest moments of the peace for me was

5

when we were at last allowed to go to a dairy and drink a glass of milk straight off. The specialists approved heartily.

.   .   .   .   .

But the other part of the specialists' advice, to forget the War : how was I to do that? How could any of us? By what effort of will could I blot out the memory of those years of flame and death, and of life in trenches that were like clay graves, and often were graves, and of wounded men trampled to death in Somme mud by a panic rush, and of seeing men killed horribly by shells, or going mad under the murderous strain.

I did my best to forget. There were hundreds of letters I had sent home. I burned nearly every one of them. There were my War diaries. There were souvenirs, maps, battalion orders, German badges, the usual trophies and mementoes. I put them away in a worn-out trunk. I had hoped to write the War history of my battalion, but it had become a task far beyond the scope of one obscure eye-witness in the ranks. It could be done only by a patient historian with access to all the official records. So for a long while I wrote no more about the War.

.   .   .   .   .

Time has healed many wounds and many minds. To-day, like many others, I am trying to remember the War I have tried so hard to forget. For I want very much to tell you about my comrades

—great-hearted comrades—many of whom did not come home. They wanted to be remembered, not as pale ghosts, but as honest, suffering soldier lads. Can I make some of them live again? Please God, I will try.

This will be my own story. I shall tell it because it is also the story of thousands upon thousands of others, not in particulars, but in broad essentials. You must forgive me for being often hazy about dates, brigade, divisions, and map references. When we were busy fighting there was no time for letter-writing or keeping a diary. True, I did make some record hour by hour of the battle of Neuve Chapelle. I was intensely anxious to record how a man felt in battle. We have all a good idea of it now, having read so many stories of the War, and talked with so many men who were in action. But it was as big an adventure as death itself then. Being an old reporter, I had my little note-book, and jotted down just how my heart began to dance with an excitement that was almost joy as the terrific bombardment opened out above us. It must have been a wonderful little record in its way, but the effort was wasted. When the battle had died out, after raging for three days, and we had had some sleep, I brought out my note-book and found the pencil had smeared illegibly through the sweat of our enormous burdens and the water in which we lay on the first night of rest. When I tried to remember it all it was impossible. I had gone through most of the battle like a sleep-walker.

·   ·   ·   ·   ·

My story will be broken and incomplete. Perhaps, under the favouritism of memory, I shall seem to make myself a hero, though I never felt like one. I must disguise some names, and in other ways save needless pain to the friends of those who broke down. Perhaps I shall excite the scorn of old comrades by getting details wrong. But at least I can do something to show you the spirit of my old battalion. That is my eager ambition, to do justice to my friends, as I sit here, on a quiet afternoon, with old War diaries and photographs about me reminding me of things forgotten. I look out on a quiet garden, under a dappled sky. Soon tea will be brought, and my little dog will wake up and ask for a saucerful, well sweetened. Friends will come in. We shall talk of the Government's future, and of the Leeds City Council, politics, and of the new books. All will be warm, cosy, companionable.

Incredible that only a few years ago I lay in a clay trench and thirsted for water on blazing midsummer days, and never thought to get back home! Incredible!

Yes, we must recall and realize the War now, lest many of us forget it wholly. At the best it is only fragments of our experience we can put together again.

CONTENTS

CONTENTS

HAUNTING YEARS

CHAPTER I

BUNDLING INTO THE ARMY

THE War was a day or two old. The scene was the swarming street outside the recruiting-office at Dundee. I struggled in a mob of old militiamen and unemployed to reach the recruiting sergeant. I was twenty-eight, unmarried, teetotal, vegetarian, a quiet, spectacled Yorkshireman. My shorthand was good, but I had never dug even a garden-bed.

A gaunt man in a muffler towered over me. He looked down, and said, not without sympathy: "Out o' work, chum?"

I was a trifle huffy. Out of work, indeed. I was News Editor (and in the Fleet Street sense, Night Editor, too) of an important morning paper, the *Dundee Advertiser*. But I could not go into that. I told the big man I had a goodish job.

"Then you make way for us lads wi'out jobs," he said.

And forthwith I was hustled back to the edge of the crowd. Funny (I thought to myself), I never knew it was so hard to become a soldier. I waited an hour or two. Still no good. I went back sorrowfully to my desk, and tried again the next day, and the next.

When the editor, friendly Alexander Urquhart, heard what I was after, he was amazed at my hopes. " You a soldier!" he said. " You couldn't stand the life for a fortnight. You'd be in hospital in a week. You could never rough it."

When he saw I was determined, he said : " If you must go, you'll have to take a commission." Again I was obstinate. I wanted to get to France quickly. I knew nothing about soldiering. The roughest militiaman knew more about it than I did. If I was to prove no good as a soldier, far better that it should be as a simple private. Command others? I was not sure I could command myself.

We knew then extraordinarily little of how a man behaves under fire. We all know now that most men can be trained to become good soldiers. Even men who are timid in civilian life may become good soldiers. When it comes to the test, they have to fight for their lives with little or no chance of getting away from it. We all fight when we have to. But in those days we had no idea whether a burst of shrapnel (we thought in terms of South African War fighting) would not make us dash off like rabbits.

See the War I must. I could not be a war correspondent. I could not get to Paris through the confusion of Northern France to join the Foreign Legion. So I decided to join a regular battalion of the British Army, one that must be in the fighting line. Men were being pressed to join the Territorials, but that was no use to me.

.   .   .   .   .   .

I tried to explain this at the recruiting-office when, after going day after day, I managed to get a dull hearing. "Don't worry, lad," I was told. "We'll get you to the Front." I warmed to the rosy old sergeant who said that. I was sent to a local drill-hall, joined an extremely mixed mob, passed the doctor, took my military oath, and remained for some days under the impression that I was a Regular, or at least a Kitchener man, a sort of temporary regular. I had been asked to help recruiting by writing for the Press, and I signed my articles, "By One of Kitchener's Hundred Thousand". Then it turned out that I was only a Territorial.

You will think this was stupid on my part. You will think it a proof that I was extraordinarily ignorant of military terms. I was, but really the mistake arose from the unprecedented confusion of recruiting-office and barracks in those days. Men were pouring in, overwhelming the ordinary staffs. Men were ready to sign anything, and say anything. They gave false names, false addresses, false ages. They suppressed their previous military service, or exaggerated it, just as seemed to promise them best. Recruits had to sign as fast as they could. They did not trouble to read their papers. Most of them were more eager in those early days about getting their food than about their commitments to King and country. Whether our motives were to defend Britain, see the War, or get free food, we bundled ourselves into the Army in those hot, wild days of August, 1914. What fun we meant to have! What fun! . . . .

My first soldiering was done at the Bell Street
Drill Hall, Dundee, amid confusion, dirt, and
noise. Those in command struggled to get things
straight, but recruits poured in, some in foul rags.
I was the first of the Bun-wallahs, those who were
supposed to be accustomed to a better diet than
others. Some of those who had been Territorials
in peace time were there to train us, but they were
mostly young, and in the first week or two regarded
the thing as a joke. We could not get uniforms
at first, and you can't make a man a soldier without
a uniform.

During the day instructors took us in small
groups for squad drill or a gentle form of physical
exercise, or for a march through the streets. About
tea-time we went off on various private pursuits,
and from about eleven o'clock men staggered in,
loaded up both outside and in with whisky and
beer. I tried to sleep in a corner, but how
could I sleep when hooligans were playing a football match up and down the centre of the hall, or
making Highland charges, yelling their fiercest?

And the dirt! Your mental picture of barracks
is of spotless, rectangular dormitories, but that
drill-hall, with all the dust, stirred up by the tramp-
ling, and with roysterers being sick at night where
they lay, and many of them prematurely lousy,
struck dismay into my heart.

We had to continue wearing civilian clothes, and
as it was a waste to wear good ones amid all that
dirt, I put on an old golf jacket and tennis shirt,
grey flannel tousers, and a pair of expensive new
fishing boots which I thought would be useful for

heavy route marches. The boots vanished after a couple of days. I asked a sergeant what I should do. " Watch yourself, laddie," he said. " They'll steal the milk out of your tea in this mob." And that was that.

In soiled garb I began to feel unhappy. I had never realized what a difference presentable clothes make to a man. I used to pay £4 for a suit in those days, a modest enough price, but one that bought more than the suit itself. It gave me self-confidence, and a certain amount of public respect. In my civilian days, as an Englishman in Dundee, I had been impressed by the general courtesy to a stranger. If I wanted information, everybody seemed anxious to oblige. I felt happy among Dundee people, but what a difference there was when I went out in shabby and dirty war clothes! The cold shoulder replaced a smiling welcome.

You young gentlemen who read this, and pride yourself that the world looks kindly upon you because of your conspicuous merit, don't be too sure. It may be that the world welcomes you, not because of your character, not because of your brains, but because your clothes make you look so well and prosperous. You would find it hard to look impressive in a shabby suit.

.   .   .   .   .

If I found many of my comrades strange. I am sure they found me stranger still. There was I with no friend at hand, a man of queer habits, a vegetarian (though I now tried hard to take Army stew, for Britain's sake), teetotal, and a queer twist of speech, for I am not Scots but pure Yorkshire, given to scribbling, and restlessly asking people how you do this and that, and what they thought of this, and how they felt when doing that. It was only my journalistic curiosity about human nature trying to make the most of these opportunities, but they thought the circumstances were suspicious. They read every day in the papers about German spies. Strange things were happening on the Tay Bridge, and even in the main streets of Dundee. There were bound to be hordes of German spies in our midst. Jove! I must be one of them. I was out of place, unwelcome, suspected. I was down in the sewers of life. What blunder had I made? Trying to sleep amid the dirt and noise and stench of foul clothes and unwashed men, I thought of my first night at school, at the old Christ's Hospital, Newgate Street, London, crying under the bed-clothes.

. . . . .

Strange things were indeed happening in the Dundee streets. People passing a tall newspaper office in Bank Street would hear terrific bangs, as though bombs had burst behind them, and would run in terror to the police and any soldiers who were about. I think it has never been disclosed before what those bangs were. They were due to the high spirits of a youth who used to fill his pockets with electric-light bulbs, go on the roof, and then drop the bulbs to crash on the pavement behind passers-by. German spies, indeed!

An order came that Captain Boase wanted to see me. I was to know him well afterwards, and to love him for his courage and unselfishness, but all I knew about him then was that he was fair game for the practical jokers. He was of anxious temperament, diffident and roundabout in his speech, and worn by the burden imposed on him in those recruiting days.

He began to question me in such a transparently guileful way that I felt an overwhelming desire to be mysterious. Our interview went something like this:

Officer: "You must forgive me if—er—I appear to be a little peremptory in my questions, a little (what shall I say?) excessive. I think you know what I mean."

W. L. A.: "Yes, sir. You mean you would like to ask me questions, and yet you don't like to ask them."

Officer: "This is a question of military duty. I shall not allow my personal wishes to interfere with my duty. I must ask you your motive in joining this battalion. Certain reports have reached me—I will not say that I place full credence in them, but these reports have reached me, I must ask you what was your motive in joining this battalion."

W. L. A.: "Must I answer this, sir? Do I understand that anything I now say may be taken down in writing and given in evidence against me in support of any future charge?"

Officer: "Well, er—. I am not asking you for confidential information."

B

W. L. A. : " Then surely I am entitled to know what the charge is."

Officer : " There is no charge. There is merely a—how shall I put it?—excited suggestion among the men that you are not what you appear to be. All I want is your assurance that you are not here for the purpose of gathering and disseminating military information."

W. L. A., with intense emphasis : " Surely, sir, you don't suspect that I am here in the pay of Germans. That would be infamous. I am British—British to the backbone."

Officer : " Yes, yes, of course, I felt sure of it. But there is so much foolish talk about German spies, that something has to be done to allay public alarm. I did not believe the suggestion against you, but I felt compelled to inquire into it. All I will ask you is to tell me of some men of standing in the town who know you and can vouch for you."

Thereupon I gave the anxious officer the names of my employers, and others, and I heard no more about the spy suggestion. I enjoyed it mightily. I felt as though I were playing the part of the injured innocent in some old-fashioned melodrama. I fear we dramatised ourselves far too much in those days. Do not blame us severely. We were young and excited, and the women's pride in us would have turned steadier heads than ours.

We had much the same spy business again a week later when an English artist, Joseph Gray, joined our battalion. He had what the Scots people call a strong English accent. He was slightly deaf. I think he was seen reading German papers, so the rumour spread that he did not understand English fully, but spoke German, and therefore must be a German.

Slowly the tumult of the drill-hall sank into something like order. After the first week or two, far more bun-wallahs joined, men who had played some part in the social and athletic life of Dundee and its neighbourhood, and whose enlistment was duly chronicled with pictures in the local press.

To my great joy, about a dozen of my old colleagues of the *Dundee Advertiser* office marched in one day. I gave up trying to transfer to a regular battalion. It seemed to me that this intolerably filthy and brainless life would now be mitigated by true comradeship. We could learn to be soldiers here, and when we were useful men it would be time to transfer to some battalion in France. I had been alone in that crowd in the drill-hall for only a few days, but I felt as strange and foreign in its midst as if I had been captured by bandits in the midst of China. I had called myself a fool again and again. I had said that prison, with its compulsory cleanness and hours to oneself, must be far better than life in the drill-hall. Now I took heart. My colleagues were the most welcome rescue-party that ever surprised a prisoner. We must keep together at all costs.

The days no longer dragged. We cleaner men were allowed to keep together. My loneliness fell away.

.   .   .   .   .

"Call this war?" said Private J. B. Nicholson,

helping himself to another chocolate from my pound box. "It's the most peaceful life I ever knew."

"Great, isn't it?" said I, shading my eyes from the hot sun, and looking across two miles of the sparkling Tay to the hills of Fife. A shimmer of heat blurred the blue-and-green landscape.

All about us on a sandy hillside were comrades of the 4th Black Watch, sleeping in peace. Blue-black kilts only half-covered brawny thighs. Black Glengarry bonnets sat askew over brown faces. Some men snored.

"Going to the Scala to-night?" asked Nicholson. "Elizabeth Craig wants the whole bunch to go—supper at her flat afterwards."

"Right-ho," I said. "I'm off on shut-eye parade. Here's the *Spectator* if you want to see it."

That was war, at home, for some of us under training, in September of 1914. An officer had marched us to the hillside, and then said: "You can lie down and go to sleep. Any man who wakes the rest by snoring will be shot at dawn. Get back to the billets by 4.15, but not before. Fall out!"

Happy days; lazy days. I remember them far better than the days of toil and death. They made rich amends for the first few days of wretchedness in the drill-hall.

.   .   .   .   .

They were days of friendship. There were about twelve of us who called ourselves, from some headline, "Writers and Fighters Too". We were all from the newspaper offices in Dundee, and meant to keep together. After the wearing discipline and incessant activity of a newspaper office, our training early in the War was like a great lark. It was just like being back at school. Responsibilities had been lifted off our shoulders. We did not worry about money, for gifts of chocolates, delicacies, cigarettes, socks, theatre tickets, magazines, books and invitations to tea poured in upon us. Learning how to quick march was kindergarten stuff after my nightly anxiety of getting a paper to press to catch trains. No longer were there those moments of sick dismay with which I realized that the rival sheet had beaten us hollow.

We had heard of the severity of military discipline, but it was nothing to that of a business office. Our main work was cleaning up the drill-hall, cleaning up our eating utensils, and cleaning up ourselves for going out. We could hardly call a route march work. It was some weeks before we got rifles to carry.

We marched out on those smiling August and September days on to country roads, halting where it pleased us best. When we bun-wallahs announced that it was time to clear the dust from our throats, a willing sergeant stopped the march and postponed training for half an hour. If we had not been eager to learn, soldiering would have been like a practical joke. But we picked up the rudiments of the job with some enthusiasm.

Joseph Lee, my old music and art critic, was senior in point of years among our Writers and

Fighters Too. I think he must have been about thirty-eight, a stalwart and stocky Scotsman, with a dark brooding head that suggested Robert Burns. He used to say his recreation was "going to and fro in the earth and walking up and down in it". He had studied art at Heatherley's and the Slade. As a young man he went to Western Canada, and I believe he was something of a cowboy. I have an impression that he tramped in Russia and was a stoker on the Black Sea. He loved music, art, Shakespeare, Burns, Scots ballads, and the drama. He had written a book of poems called "Tales o' Our Town", and a play, "Fra Lippo Lippi", and he had produced and acted in plays.

Dear old Joe! He was (and is) a great character. The time came when, except for the Colonel, he must have been the best-loved man in the battalion. There was nothing Joe would not do for a comrade if it was in his power. Above all, when in France, he kept us cheerful in our platoon, because when he was with us, no matter how filthy was the trench scene and how nauseous its smells of the dead and its butcher duties, he never let us forget the background of civilized life: he was our link with great minds and great art and the pure pleasures of the mind.

Our tea-parties might be more gormondizing without him, mere physical pleasures, but when Joe was there he arranged everything like a chef and an artist. He had countless merry tales of rough life and stage life, and he would sing us songs of the North, not in a big voice, but with husky sweetness. He and I and young J. B. Nicholson made an inseparable three. Nick, hardly yet a man, thinnish and brooding, was a son of the manse, with an eager, phrase-seeking mind. Women called him "Poor Nick" in those days, with somewhat of a sigh, for he was a gentle soul, and in his fineness seemed all unarmed against the rough contacts of the barracks. He had a sweet, artless way. One day the Regimental Sergeant-Major stopped him with a bark as he was entering the officers' mess. "Who gave you permission to go in there?" he roared, for to him the officers' mess was as sacred as the high altar in a cathedral. Nick was unconscious of impiety. "That's quite all right, Major," he said. "I've been put on guard to-night, and I'm going to ask the Colonel to let me use his telephone to put off an appointment."

What can you do with such innocence? The R.S.M., though a grizzled old regular of the fire-and-brimstone tradition, must have liked that slim lad eager to speak to his girl. He told him to go and ring up from a public call-office, and gave him a pass to leave the drill-hall.

Yes, it was just like school again, with intense friendships, an instant breaking into talk and fun when lessons were over for the time being, endless arguments about the future, and about all that agitated the mind of youth in those days : how much was genuine in spiritualism, and what it meant, whether the British Empire would go the way of Rome, whether we must become Protectionist, and how we could see the world and become famous.

The change from the old routine broadened us

physically. It also broadened us, or, rather, loosened us mentally. Most of our little crowd were determined not to go back to the old life in Dundee. We felt we had been released from it for ever. Some of us had.

Many outside the drill-hall behaved as though the War were a gigantic merry-making. There was the excited and careless spirit of crowds at a royal wedding. The music-halls and the dance-halls were crammed. Commercially, the War was a good thing for sandbag-making Dundee, and there was plenty of money about. The War news in our own papers looked cheerful. I remember a small message came reporting that the Germans had given way in one part of the Western theatre of war, and prisoners had shown the influence of drink. A great newspaper banner line proclaimed on the strength of this:

GERMAN ARMY STAGGERING HOME
DRUNK AND DISORDERLY.

The only casualty that came near to us was that of one of my printers, a reservist, who was killed in the unfortunate effort to defend Antwerp. It had not yet occurred to us that War was an exceedingly dangerous occupation. Mr. Lloyd George was then making picturesque recruiting speeches, and I remember in one of them he said that of those who went to the Front only a tiny fraction would come to any hurt, while the rest would return to be held in honour all their days. I cannot at this distance of time profess to remember the words, but that was his point. We all believed it.

We were young gallants in those days, with troops of friends, a smile from every girl we knew, and from many we didn't, and an enviable feeling of fitness. After a few weeks Nick and I were dispatched to train under canvas near Monifieth, on the windy Firth of Tay. There we learnt how to fire a rifle, and something of extended drill movements. We did bayonet drill to music. We charged up hills, and drank enormous quantities of tea and lemonade. Soon we were trained men and passed for guard duty. For a time we served in a large house taken over at Broughty Ferry, close to an ancient stump of a castle that looks out on the Tay. Here our company commander was Captain Boase. He was most anxious for our comfort, and helped us to transform the lounge into what we proudly termed the Pink Palace. Joe Lee supervised its decoration with pictures.

We bun-wallahs did not draw our rations cooked, preferring to receive our meat raw and take it to a local pastrycook, who turned it into meat pies, and added vegetables and sweetmeats at some small expense. We clubbed together to buy respectable cutlery, and were astonished when Captain Boase told us it was bad taste for us to differentiate ourselves in that way from the rougher men. It was our duty to eat exactly what the others ate and in the same way. We listened with some indignation. Then one of us found ironic tongue. " Very good, sir," he said, " and shall we modify our table manners, too?"

I forget how the discussion went on, but after that we drew our Army stew like the rest and ate it from tins. Perhaps Captain Boase was right. It did not matter very much. We were soon to be beyond the reach of table refinements.

We had begun to take soldiering more seriously. We had a pride in our handling of arms. But in many ways we still had civilian habits of mind. Some important officer was inspecting us one day and had a look down Joe Lee's rifle. "Filthy," he said in a voice of thunder. "Oh, no," said Joe, easily, "I think you'll find it's only a little superficial dust."

The same officer demanded of me why I had turned up on parade with a muddy kilt. I replied in my gentle English voice, "I am afraid I must have stepped into a puddle on the way here."

In a real soldier those replies would have been insolence. On our lips they were innocence.

The first Christmas of the War and its companion Scots festival, Hogmanay, brought us much hospitality. Our company had its Christmas dinner at the air station, Carolina Port, on the Tay. It was the usual stew, but an English officer, Lieutenant Gladstone, a kinsman of the great statesman, provided Christmas pudding. Our real feasting was on Hogmanay, when we had turkey bridies (Scots for pies), Christmas pudding, and beer. It was all very well, but the effect of goodwill was spoiled by the fact that armed sentries were placed at the doors to keep us in. Hogmanay (the last day of the year) was celebrated with much drinking by many Scots people in those days. I remember a time when on Hogmanay you might find girls lying drunk on the pavement. Those were the days of Drunken Scotland. In spite of the precautions of our officers some of the men escaped from the air station and took part in carousals. For us Writer-Fighters there were the delightful continued hospitalities of warm-hearted Baillie (now Sir William) and Mrs. High and Mr. and Mrs. J. B. Clark.

Soon after this I was given a long week-end leave, which I spent in Glasgow seeing old Yorkshire friends. I went off very early in the morning and had breakfast on the train. When I was halfway through my bacon and eggs a naval officer came in. He said nothing to me, but told the attendant that he must turn me out, since an officer could not have breakfast in the same dining-car as a lance-corporal. The attendant was a little sarcastic. " Couldn't he really, sir?" he said. Thereupon he came over to me and said : " Come into the kitchen, Jock. I'll give you the finest breakfast there you ever had." Nor would he let me pay for it. I find that I wrote on 8th February in my diary : " Generally believed that we are for the Front soon. No inclination to meditate upon the prospect. Suppose I shall probably be killed with many good comrades, but cannot realize it. I am not devil-may-care, but fatalistic. Will cross the bridge when I come to it. Much more interested in my old paper than in what fighting will be like. My one fear is lest I should turn out to be a coward."

Before we reached the Front there was one more phase of soldiering to go through. The battalion had taken over some of the guard duties for the Tay defences. My company, or at any rate, my platoon, was sent to Wormit, on the Fife side of the river, to guard the bridge. This was a little village that deserved a jollier name. It clambered up and down a leafy hill-side. We were billeted in people's homes, and, as it was a residential resort for some of the more prosperous business people of Dundee, we were entertained most hospitably.

I was exceptionally fortunate, being treated as an honoured guest by a most gracious hostess, but I had a jolt at the start. A sharply-spoken maid said : " If you're coming in here, soldier, you've got to be clean. You can have as many baths as you like, but if we find you dirty, out you go." Happily, I passed Minnie's test of cleanliness, and within a day or two the good girl was insisting on cleaning my rifle and equipment for me.

" But when are we going to get to the Front?" the impatient reader will be asking. Yes, my friends. It is just what we were asking all through those months.

Just before we left I had the good fortune to become engaged—very happily engaged.

CHAPTER II

OFF TO FRANCE

WE were off to France, a whole proud battalion. Off to France! We were bright-eyed with excitement: our hearts danced for joy.

It was February, 1915. The ambition that had swayed us since August, 1914, the ambition for which we had left our homes, our wives, our sweethearts, our good civilian pay, our warm beds, was to reach its long-delayed fulfilment.

What were our emotions in that hour? Who shall reveal the dazzling hopes and the wormy fears hidden in each man's heart? At times, as I walked alone, kilt swinging gaily, there came upon me a dread of what was to come. How could I take the life of another man, some decent, honest man, and leave him torn flesh like railway-smash victims I had seen in my reporting days?

A bronzed old Regular sergeant, good old Callary, was a great comfort. I told him of my dread. "God bless you, laddie," he said with great heartiness, "you've no call to worry like that. You'll think no more of putting your bayonet through a man than of putting your finger in a pot of jam. Fighting comes as natural as eating." It was comforting to know that. I half-believed it.

The excitement of the last day in Scotland swept away the sombre shadows at the back of the mind. Off to France! The nearness of danger gave us an exciting, enormous feeling of completed manhood.

I believe one or two wasters vanished, to join elsewhere some other unit that was not so likely to move off to France, but it is sober fact that almost all of us were longing fiercely to get to the Front. Even what we had heard of the hardships of the Retreat from Mons, sometimes from the lips of wounded men, did not chasten our spirits. We envied those indomitable fighters their place in history.

There is a school of war-writing that derides those simple and honest emotions of ours, makes a mock of our eagerness to serve and our readiness to do our duty, and sees us only as poor, wretched animals, caught and tormented in a gigantic cage of steel and flame. It was not so in February, 1915.

What made us still more eager to go to France was that our local rivals, the Fifth Battalion of the Black Watch, Forfarshire Territorials, had left the British Isles as early as 29th October, 1914, and had received much honour in the local papers. We wanted to show what our own battalion could do.

It was 23rd February, 1915. The Battalion received the order to go to France on active service. Events jostled each other hard. There were dashes to the telephones. Telegrams. Train-time rumours. Inspections. Farewells. Good wishes. Loading up. A breathless, happy rush.

Fake messages from the cookhouse that all was cancelled. Men shouting " This way for England, France, Belgium and Berlin."

.   .   .   .   .

Our march to the station and the scenes there were of an excitement never to be known in peacetime. The streets were crowded all the way, for this was a city going to war. The pipes of the Sixth Black Watch played "Hielan' Laddie" (the Black Watch march past) and "Happy we've been a' thegither". It was impossible to keep military formation. The women were kissing their men. Factory girls in their shawls broke in among us. A red-headed girl flung her arms about me. " Glory be to Jesus," she cried again and again. Everyone pressed gifts upon us. But a few of the women from mean streets were sobbing. Useless for us to tell them that we were only to guard lines of communications. The women in the mean streets know by tradition what war is. And perhaps their own men were dead already.

Every journalist in Dundee was at the station to see the Writer-Fighters off. One of them, as the train started, called out the sub-editors' nightly cry to reporters, " Keep it short!"

We travelled in unexpected comfort to Southampton, embarked in the s.s. *Rosetti*, and lay anchored opposite Netley Hospital for a night and a day. We had with us on board a draft of three hundred Scots Guardsmen, magnificent in physique. We eyed them diffidently. These were the very gods of war.

We sailed at 6 p.m. on the twenty-fifth. I was down in the bottom of the hold, in a sort of cattle pen. It was a night of misery, as we crouched there on our packs, in the dark the whole time. Dawn, Havre, and breakfast revived us. Soon we were marching with skirling pipes and swinging kilts up a steep hill to a rest camp. On the way a schoolmaster called his children to their feet and they sang to us, in English, "God Save the King". A day in camp; then we went by train to Lillers, about twelve miles behind the Armentières-La Bassée sector of the British front. Thence we marched to Calonne, on the Lys, and our platoon slept in a barn. The sun shone. Life in this rustic haunt, though it was only ten miles behind the firing, was cheerful. We wrote dozens of letters, wandered about the little village, tried our French on the natives, watched the aeroplanes and listened to the muffled thud of guns.

The only thing that had irked us so far was the enormous load we had to carry. We had been given all sorts of comforts, woollen things, and so forth, and staggered along, as the phrase went, like decorated Christmas-trees.

Poor Skerry, an Englishman who had been my foreign sub-editor, was the first to rebel. Though we had orders not to take off our equipment, he threw his off his back and said they could shoot him for it. The example spread. We flung away everything we could dispense with. It must have been rare treasure for the inhabitants.

CHAPTER III

WE marched next to Richebourg St. Vaast, where we found ourselves part of the Bareilly Brigade in the Meerut Division of the Indian Army Corps. It seemed romantic that we were to live and fight alongside the Indian battalions. We had read much about the Gurkhas, those hardy, cheerful little fellows. And we were delighted to find ourselves brigaded with the 2nd Black Watch, a Regular battalion, which was to teach us our job.

Our first lessons were exciting; we had to supply working and carrying parties for the line. Whilst in billets at Richebourg we saw shell after shell plumping into the church tower, stood in the streets to watch, and cheered derisively, but when we were stumbling through muddy fields by night, dropping every few yards over a telephone wire, or having the long rifle we then carried caught in wire head-high, enemy fire was more terrifying.

On our first journey to the trenches we halted for a time against the wall of a farm building. No sooner had we lain down than bullets began to whizz just over us and struck sparks on a wall. It was as if we had been seen. We were assured the Germans could not possibly see us. They were firing blindly. But it was hard to persuade

33

C

ourselves that the next bullet would not drop just a little lower and end a promising career. In fact, we could not persuade ourselves on that point. We felt sure that the bullets were fired by Germans behind our own lines and that they knew much more about us than we knew about them. There had been Germans left behind to conceal themselves in haystacks, and we believed some of these were still sniping.

We felt safer when we reached the communication trenches, and had to crush along these narrow alleys until we came to waiting 2nd Black Watch men, and dumped our loads of rations and ammunitions with them. Then back as fast as we could go.

．　　　．　　　．　　　．　　　．

I remember a night when we had to dig a length of trench, in preparation, though we did not know it, for the battle of Neuve Chapelle. The Germans now and then sent a shell over in our direction. It did not arrive with anything like the thud to which we were accustomed. There would be a rapidly approaching and loudening whine, then a great blinding flash of red, and the most vicious gnashing sound of explosion you could imagine. There was something incredibly malevolent about its force. We were very frightened, but no one was hurt, and we worked on physically shaken but doing our utmost to control wavering nerves. Our excitement was not wholly controllable. Several of us, Nick and I among them, were sick.

When we went to take our first turn of duty

in the front line we did not experience anything
like the same terror. A cover gives you a feeling
of security out of all proportion to the actual shelter
it affords. We were afraid of being sniped or
shelled whilst we were moving out over the open,
but once in the communication trench we felt we
had only to duck to avoid the German missiles.
We had the same feeling of protection later if we
crouched beneath a waterproof sheet stretched
across a trench corner.

My chief memory of that first night in the front
line is of intense cold about our feet. There was
a good deal of water in the trench. We of the
4th Black Watch were intermingled with Regulars
of the 2nd, whose business was to show us how to
do things. There were no dug-outs for us, and
when not on sentry duty we sat huddled upon the
fire-step, the ledge on which you stood to shoot
over the trench parapet. One of our sergeants
had brought a good supply of rum, and he was
very hospitable with this to the Regulars. My
companion was a hairy, hard-bitten veteran of the
Old Bill type. He had little to say, and this was
as well, for I could not understand his gruff Scots
tongue. He had nip after nip of the warming
spirit, and grew more and more genial. The
sergeant seemed to forget that he was in a post of
danger. He was lost in a world of illusion.

This began to alarm me as dawn approached. It
was then that the Germans would attack, if at all,
taking advantage of the last patches of darkness to
crawl over, and then be on us when they could see
their way, and would find us at our dullest after

the strain of the night. I declined the rum myself, being in those days a teetotaller, and much impressed by the *Spectator* campaign in favour of downing glasses. Towards dawn an officer came round to ask if all was well. I was afraid Old Bill, who by this time was quite cheerful with rum, would get into trouble, but at the sound of the officer's voice he stiffened into military woodenness, and his "Nothing to report, sir", spoken whilst his face was turned towards the unseen enemy, was a masterpiece of emotionless routine.

I grew more and more alarmed as I kept bobbing my head up to look over the parapet for an instant, for I had not then learnt that in the dark it was safe to look steadily over the parapet as long as one did not move when a flare was up. The light grew, showing up before long two dead Germans, whom Old Bill had warned me to look for. Then to my amazement I saw soldiers in front of us no more than twenty yards away. My heart gave a great bound. By this time Old Bill was snoring.

I called to Nicholson. " Ought we to fire?"

Nick thought we ought, but, it seemed an awful thing to raise our rifles and shoot dead those unknown men out there. I had never had the heart to shoot a rabbit. It was a ghastly thought that I might now have to execute those men on the other side of the parapet. We had another peep. The men seemed to be doing nothing in particular. Some were lying down.

One of our own officers came along. We told him there were Germans just in front. He looked incredulous. We bade him take a look for himself. "Good God!" he said, "those aren't Germans. That's one of our own listening-posts."

It must have been somebody's business to warn us of that listening-post out there, and somebody must have forgotten to do so. We had been on guard all night, unconscious that our own men were in No Man's Land in front. Nick and I had nearly fired on our comrades. We felt utterly green. We wanted to do things, to take the initiative, but there we were stuck in a trench pool all night, and on the point of murdering our friends. I vowed that come what might I would not drink rum on duty.

.   .   .   .   .

We raw beginners were soon to know the bewilderments of battle. Five days after we had first seen the trenches the battalion fought in its first action. We were fumbling amateurs. And only a little while before we had been told that our saluting was disgraceful, and our appearance most unsoldierly. A general had reviewed us with evident distaste, and there had been a furious reprimand for us all because men had gone on parade without being shaved. One of the sergeants of my company was the chief offender. He meant no harm. He had assumed that we had come to France to fight, and not to be dandies, and he appeared on that dreadful parade looking like one of the hairy veterans in a Crimean picture. The general must have been severe upon the colonel.

Shame and disgrace changed our happy atmosphere.

The second-in-command, Major Muir, came to our company to read the Riot Act. He was a prosperous coal merchant in civil life, and of an easy-going, generous temperament. When we were shivering under canvas on the banks of the Tay, he had allowed us to help ourselves from his trucks. But now he appeared with a long and resentful face (small blame to him), and told us how little we knew of soldiering, and how important it was to salute properly and to appear clean and smart and shaved on parade.

This was shocking news. We thought we had done for ever with drills, punctilious saluting, and shaving before breakfast. That was the most complete and pathetic of our many illusions at that time. We were to learn that however feebly we might wield the rifle and bayonet, and though we might throw bombs like schoolgirls, we must be superbly efficient with the razor. We could not win the War with hairy chins. The inspecting generals were sure of that.

CHAPTER IV

THE BATTLE OF NEUVE CHAPELLE

IN the midst of our humiliations came word that we were wanted for a smash at the foe, a really big effort. This was a surprise to us all, but rumour quickly spread an explanation. It was said there had been a small Indian mutiny; one of the white officers was a German in disguise, who had led his men off to the other side.

I never heard of anything to confirm this story, but it is worth mentioning as an example of trench and billet rumours. Be on your guard against some of the sensational things you read in war books. Stories like that were endless, and there was no chance to verify them. It may be that some of the things I describe never happened. I am merely telling you what I was told, and what I believed, but you must understand that I was not going about like a reporter, getting every statement confirmed. Thus on one of our early turns of duty in the trenches word was passed round of a cruel death. It was said one of our men had carelessly thrown a tin or a paper on top of a dug-out. An officer found what he had done, and ordered him to go on to the dug-out and bring the offensive tin or paper down. This meant exposing the man to grave danger, for it was daylight, the Germans were only about eighty yards away, and snipers were bound to shoot. The officer, threatening the

man, made him go after the rubbish, and the
Germans promptly shot him dead. Such was the
story. Was it true? I cannot say. I never met
anybody who claimed to have seen it, but it was
generally believed among us.

We felt honoured to think we had been chosen
to serve in battle. Some of those who did not go to
France till much later may think I am writing just
the conventional journalistic phrase of the period.
But no; we were eager to fight, to prove ourselves
comrades and helpers to the Old Contemptibles,
of whom we had heard so glorious a record, and
our regular friends of the Indian Army. We were
smarting to avenge the things said to us, and to
show that even a man with hairs on his chin might
have no spot on his military record. We were eager
to live up to the reputation of our famous regiment.

Later, before going into a charge, we generally
shook hands, and promised each other that the
survivors would send messages to the bereaved.
But nothing so mournful was in our mood then.
We were excited and eager to do that for which
we had joined the Army, our sworn duty. Moreover, there was the thrilling anticipation of being
in at the great final victory of the War. Vain
hope! Vain, ridiculous hope, as we see it now!
In those days we thought we had but to break
through the German front, and the enemy, short
of men, would crumple up. This was not the mere
ignorant opinion of raw Territorial privates. It
was the professed hope of the Army Commander,
General Sir Douglas Haig, who, in a special order
dated March 9th, said:

TO THE 1ST ARMY.

We are about to engage the enemy under very favourable conditions. Until now in the present campaign the British Army has, by its pluck and determination, gained victories against an enemy greatly superior in men and guns.

Reinforcements have made us stronger than the enemy in our front. Our guns are now more numerous than the enemy's are, and are also larger than any hitherto used by any army in the field.

Our Flying Corps has driven the enemy from the air.

We are now about to attack with about forty-eight battalions a locality in that front which is held by some three German battalions. It seems probable, also, that for the first day of the operations the Germans will not have more than four battalions available for the counter-attack.

Quickness of movement is therefore of first importance to enable us to forestall the enemy and thereby gain success without severe loss.

At no time in the War has there been a more favourable moment for us, and I feel confident of success. The extent of that success must depend on the rapidity and determination with which we advance.

To ensure success each one of us must play his part and fight like men for the honour of Old England,

We studied the message. "Three cheers!" said Nick. "We've done with trenches."

"Yes, if we break through and get them on the run, and don't let them stop," said I, sagely. We thought we saw it clearly. It was all so simple. We were to make a surprise attack with a battering-ram of men and guns, and once we had thrust it through the trench system the foe would be rolled up. Yes, rolled up: it was a favourite phrase then.

Later battles were more mysterious, and the private rarely knew what was happening except in his own bits of battle-field. He and a chum might get stuck in a reeking pit for a whole day and night, and not know whether friend or foe was in that smashed trench fifty yards away. But we had a good idea at Neuve Chapelle of what we were after.

For one thing, the field of battle was tiny. My recollections may be wrong, but I think we expected to make a gap of only two miles or so. We had a very fair idea of the ground to be covered. We Territorials, eager for our first battle, studied it as much as we could.

Neuve Chapelle, which gave the battle its name, was a little village with a church and a brewery. It was close to the main road that ran from Estaires, which was in our hands, to cross-roads made by the Rue du Bois, where lay a dug-out position we called Port Arthur, then across to the German front line, and so on to La Bassée, which was occupied by the Germans. Neuve Chapelle had changed hands several times in the autumn, and was held by the Germans from the beginning of November throughout the winter, making an awkward dent in our front line. Behind Neuve Chapelle, as we faced the enemy, lay a little wood, the Bois du Biez. The ground slowly rose towards the village of Aubers, and about nine miles beyond was the great city of Lille. Our object was to straighten out the salient, get to the high ground, especially at Aubers Ridge, and there command the approaches to the important manufacturing towns of Lille, Roubaix, and Tourcoing.

We were hopeful enough to believe that on the night of the battle there would be cosy billets for us in Lille.

But even raw Territorials could see our task was none too easy. Our trenches were only for temporary shelter. We never meant to settle in them. The enemy had made fortifications of his, with places in which to sleep in comfort. Moreover, a battered village like Neuve Chapelle could be made extremely strong with sandbag protections. We had seen that already at Richebourg, where we laughed at the shells falling around our billets.

Then we should have to fight our way across fields so sodden with winter rains that they were like morasses. Before the battle we had to throw bridges across drains and watercourses in order to enable a concentration of troops to be made quickly. Communication breastworks were made, for communication trenches would quickly have filled with water. We dragged our way up with ammunition, bombs, rations, sandbags, barbed wire, spare bridges, plans, hurdles, and pickets, and stored them at depots in the fields. Knowing the time it took to do this on our side of the line, what were we to expect when we crossed to the German fields with no multiplication of bridges to help us over the watery parts, and all our fighting material to be carried forward?

Our best hope was that we should take the enemy by surprise, blot out his front line with an overwhelming artillery bombardment, then sweep through as fast as we could go. Once in his open country we should face conditions that were as bad for him as for us. Everything, then, seemed to turn on the possibility of surprise. Could we catch the German off his guard?

As the day for the battle approached we looked skyward with the utmost anxiety. It would be impossible to conceal our preparations from German airmen. Fortunately for us our own airmen were then extremely powerful. They challenged the German planes, and it was obvious even to a simple private that we had command of the air in that section for the time being.

The battle plans, of course, were not revealed to humble people like myself, then a lance-corporal. Men of this rank, the one just above that of private, were not in the confidence of majors, let alone major-generals. But it was clear to me from the lie of the land, from the assembly of ammunition and engineering material, and from the hope of getting to Lille, that we were in for a tremendous shattering struggle. True, before we had Haig's message, one of the Writer-Fighters of our little group said it would be only a small biff, never mentioned in the papers. He said such attacks were constantly being made, and nothing was said about them. Joe Lee, Nick and I all held the big battle theory. We were convinced this was the battle that might end the War.

Not that we had much time for conversation in those days. We had become sweating coolies. We were carrying all through the hours of darkness, every night. How we came to loathe the sodden tracks, with wire overhead, wire underfoot, every few yards! We had always to carry our rifles and ammunition with us, not because there was any danger of our being suddenly attacked, but because that is the military way. We should have been more useful without them, but no, that was against the military code.

We panted and cursed, and our muscles ached as we struggled on, hour after hour, with burdens that made our hearts do queer things. We snapped at each other. Nick, who was fond of the medical dictionary, assured us our shortness of breath, irregular action of the heart, and extreme irritability, were due to our being taxed beyond our physical capacity. He mournfully prophesied that at the end of our days we should be suffering from a functional affection of the heart. We could not help quarrelling on those nightmare carrying parties. Nick would curse me for not warning him of a telephone wire that whipped into his face. Then he would be overcome with remorse. " Forgive me, Linton," he would say. " Don't take any notice of my symptoms. It's only a functional affection. The real affection for you is still there."

Joe Lee and I carried our burdens fairly well, but it was a killing struggle for Nick, who, I suppose, was only about twenty-one, tall, but of slight build, and not of athletic habit. In those hours of trial we cursed ourselves for not having sought commissions. Yet had we suddenly been offered them, and invited to take the next train home for a cadet course, we should have refused. We were going into the biggest battle that had ever been fought, the battle that was to end the War, the battle that would outshine Trafalgar and Waterloo. We had to be there. We were proud to be there.

"We've done the donkey work," said Nick. "It would be a damned shame if they didn't put us in the front stalls to see the show."

"Yes," someone added, "we'll show if we are Saturday afternoon soldiers"—referring to a gibe in pre-War days at Territorials.

So the day came, and still the enemy, as far as we could see, was blind to our battle preparations. We might be raw, but we were keen, intelligent men, all volunteers. The wasters and the the criminals had been kicked out of the battalion or deserted in Scotland. We meant to do our best for the honour of the Black Watch, the pride of Dundee. We felt that loving eyes at home were upon us.

Bewilderments were to come, but not yet the bleak misery, the all-but suicidal desolations of the Somme and Passchendaele.

It was the night of March the 9th, 1915. Snow swept down upon us in the flooded trenches near Neuve Chapelle. We grew colder and colder. I never thought I could be so chilled and still live. It was a biting torture for the body.

We could hardly drag our feet along when orders came to move from the trench to the Port Arthur dug-outs, there to snatch a few hours' sleep before we began battle.

These dug-outs were welcome only by contrast with wet trenches. They were poor make-shifts of mud huts, often with ground-sheet for roof. They could not withstand bombardment, but they were some shelter from the weather. We huddled in with numbed wits. There was a young runner (a messenger) of the 2nd Black Watch in a dug-out where I was put. He shivered at my side, and stammered.

" It's n-n-not that I'm afraid, Corporal," he exclaimed. " It's the c-c-cold. We've only c-c-come lately from India. I'm all right, chum, but I just c-c-can't help it. D-d-do you m-mind v-very much?" I said no, I quite understood, it was purely physical, like my being sick the first time under fire.

The phase "purely physical" gave the lad great comfort. He used it several times as we talked. We became good friends in those hours of waiting for the battle. He was a brave little fellow, and anxious not to give a bad impression to a Territorial. His battalion was in billets near ours. Some months later I saw him wearing a D.C.M.

ribbon, for continuing to carry messages though buried several times by shell-fire.

At 5 a.m. my platoon comrades and I were rooted out to move to a reserve trench. We shambled over ground hardened with frost. It was colder than ever.

We called it a trench, but it was nothing like the fortified cuttings that became familiar later. It was more of a breastwork, a stockade strengthened with sandbags of earth. Joe Lee, Nicholson, and I were together, sitting close to each other, backs to the stockade. Dawn came, and we peered across at the German lines, wondering if Jerry knew we were coming.

At 7 a.m. a German flew out of a low-lying cloud, swooped over Port Arthur, and after coming down to three or four hundred feet, whence he must have been able to see our lines crowded, he raced back. Now we were for it. German guns began, but directed their fire against the Port Arthur trenches, which we had left. Except for our usual morning hate with registering guns at dawn, the British artillery held its fire until 7.30 a.m. Then began, after a single shot that appeared to be a signal, the hell fury of bombardment from 480 guns and howitzers. The noise almost split our numbed wits. As the shells went over our heads we grew more and more excited. We could not hear each other. Shots from the eighteen pounders were screaming not far over our heads, and much higher up, higher than the highest mountain of Europe, high explosives from the 15-inch howitzers were rushing like express trains. After a while we could trace the different sounds.

There was no difficulty in making out the German trenches. They had become long clouds of smoke and dust, flashing continuously with shell-bursts, and with enormous masses of trench material and bodies sailing high above the smoke cloud. The purely physical effect on us was one of extreme exhilaration. We could have laughed and cried with excitement. We thought that bombardment was winning the War before our eyes. Incredible that the men in the German front line could have escaped. We felt sure we were going to pour through the gap.

Looking towards the village of Neuve Chapelle we saw the houses terribly battered, but not crumbled away as we expected. We thought the German artillery must have been swept out of existence. Vain hope. Counter fire opened upon us.

"They're shelling our fellows," Nicholson exclaimed, in extreme surprise. They were. We looked along the breastwork and saw about 300 yards away shrapnel plumping among our Black Watch Terriers. Stretcher-bearers ran along the line. Shell after shell came over, each about ten yards nearer Nicholson and myself. But a few minutes and our turn would come. We had no thought of escape. We had to lie and wait whilst the punctual shells worked along the line. "This looks like the end," said Nick.

On my right lay a young architect, Douglas

D

Bruce, who had crept up to us for warmth. "Och," he said, "if we're for it we're for it."

It was the nearest we had yet been to death, and we were surprised at our calm. (We had then seen little killing at close quarters.)

Death was ruling a straight line along our trench. Crash! Crash! Crash! Our turn was coming. Now the line was vering slightly beyond our trench. The shells were falling five yards behind the breastwork, six yards, seven yards, eight yards.

"The next one's ours," said Nick. "Good luck, Linton." We shook hands. We wormed as low as we could. The shell came screaming. It burst ten yards away with a great gnashing roar. Earth drenched us. There was a cry of astonishment and pain at my side, while yet the up-thrown earth was falling.

"Damn them!" said Douglas Bruce very heartily. His mouth was bleeding. He had had a whack on the jaw, and a tooth had been knocked out. He took it calmly.

"Stretcher-bearers," we cried, and a man crept up and did what he could.

The shrapnel passed along the line, growing more and more harmless as it fell further behind the trench. Then it stopped, all was quiet, and a lark sang. Bruce started to walk with bloody jaw on the first stage of a journey that was to take him back to Scotland.

An order came shouted along. "4th Black Watch, move to the left in single file."

It was 11 a.m. The village of Neuve Chapelle had been taken with the bayonet, and we were ordered to move forward to the captured German trenches. We passed many Indian dead and stinking shell-pits.

There was a point at which we had to jump a ditch. As we jumped we were in full view of the Germans. They were a longish way off, but now and then hit a man as he jumped. Our company commander, Captain Boase, on the other side of the ditch, called on us to hurry. We were bunching slightly as men hesitated to jump. I remember four in front of me. The first ran as fast as he could, and jumped high. Crack! He was wounded slightly, but carried on. Then a little stumpy fellow, as he jumped, was shot dead, his knees sagging as he fell. The next man, oldish and heavy, just flopped into the ditch itself and scrambled out unhurt. Then Nicholson rushed it safely.

Now for it. I took a good run, aimed to jump high, tucked my legs under me, then thrust them forward for the landing, just as though I were jumping for Peele B House at my old school, Christ's Hospital. Bullets whistled past, but all was well.

Curious that that jump stands out so clearly in my memory. I cannot think what happened next, except that there seemed to be more and more fire, and the situation was more and more confused, and the stench of the shell-pits stung the nostrils.

I remember seeing one of our men flop before

a shell-burst. He rose covered with earth, and made towards me white with passion, his eyes rolling. " This is madness!" he cried. " The world's gone mad. Why don't you stop it?"
" Wish I could," I said.
" It's murder," he went on. " Why don't the papers stop it?"
I spoke soothingly, but he said the same things over and over again, and went off raging.
I remembered being stationed with my section, probably after some hours, to guard a pump at a brewery. As we moved to it we passed a notice-board still standing with the word "Danger". Nicholson laughed as if it were the greatest joke of the War. By this time I was too tired to laugh. I was stupid with fatigue, cold, and strain.
The brewery had been severely battered, but was now quiet. Nick and I stood under a wall trying to follow the battle. We saw an English battalion, I think the Leicesters, going into a charge. We were near enough to see butchers' cleavers and hatchets hanging from some men's belts. They moved slowly, the ground being soft with its churning up by shells, in spite of the frost. Though here and there men fell, they kept a straight line. As a man fell his companions drew nearer to close the gap. I remember Nicholson, greatly excited, saying: " Did you ever see anything like it? It's magnificent." But I did not watch the end. I sank down exhausted. I felt sick. My head was on fire with pain.
We seemed to be forgotten in that smoking

brewery where the lyddite still stunk. After a while a shell roared at us, went red with fury, and smashed the pump like a maniac. My occupation was gone. How could I be said to be guarding a pump that no longer existed? I looked at the remains with heavy pathos.

Leaving a man on guard, I hunted about for a Black Watch officer. I saw Captain Boase ducking and stumbling in No Man's Land, and went towards him. He told me he had found two wounded men, and asked if I had seen any R.A.M.C. fellows. I had, at the brewery. I took him to them, but when he asked if they could bring in the wounded they said it was too dangerous, and not their job anyway. One man had been shot in trying to reach them.

" We'll do it," Nick and I said, and Joe Lee and young Paton, coming up, volunteered also. We borrowed a stretcher, and, with Captain Boase leading, ran out to the wounded men. We brought in a German first, a Bavarian, all bloody about the thighs. The poor wretch had been wounded on patrol. He was heavy to carry, but we got him to the brewery. He was intensely relieved to be picked up, and shook hands with us all several times, having no English and we having no German.

Then we brought in the Englishman. He was very quiet, almost unconscious. There was a good deal of rifle fire about us, but no one was hit.

I felt better now. It was best to be doing something. And I began in those moments to respect

Captain Boase in a way I had never done before.
He had seemed a little too anxious at home, not
ready enough to trust a man to do the decent and
proper thing, but here he was master of himself,
a good Samaritan, a true officer. I was ready to
follow him anywhere.

I asked him what we were to do next. You
will see that I was still the civilian, in spite of my
khaki uniform : the real soldier would have waited
for orders.

He said one of our companies had had heavy
casualties in capturing a snipers' house, and our
bombardment had not done all the damage we
expected. Ammunition was running short, and
probably we should be wanted either to carry
ammunition up or take a German trench by assault.
Meanwhile I was to keep my section at the brewery
and await orders.

Leaving a man on duty, Nick and I wandered
about to see what was to be seen. Men lay dead
along the battered German trench. Our shells had
done unimaginable harm. A German officer's
body had been cut in two, and the upper half had
fallen into the British front-line trench.

An Indian's head had been blown off, and was
not to be found, but the most harrowing sights of all
to us were those of young soldiers of the 2nd Black
Watch, looking pathetically young in their blue-
black kilts, and with the gay bloom of the red
hackle in their bonnets.

An Indian boy came rushing over towards us,
whirling a bicycle round and round his head. We
thought he meant to assault us, but he was grinning

and laughing as hard as he could. We tried to soothe him with the soldier Esperanto: " Teek teek, Johnny. Allyman no bon." We made no impression upon him. He was out of his mind.

CHAPTER V

ORDERS came to report for carrying duties, and as dusk came these tasks were redoubled. As night came Nick and I stood for a moment in No Man's Land, looking at a great red blaze that completed the conventional battle landscape. It was the trees of the Bois du Biez, set ablaze by the artillery.

We carried, and ached, and cursed, and carried. The sergeants in the front line were insatiable for more ammunition.

For a time, though I cannot say when, we found ourselves back at the dug-outs at Port Arthur. I lay down in one with Nick and Joe Lee. A familiar voice, that of Major Wauchope, nephew of the famous general of the South African War, was there receiving reports. A runner would come up and say in a breathless, broad Scots voice: " Lieutenant So-and-so has been killed, sir, and second-lieutenant has been badly wounded, but we've got him down to the first-aid post."

Major Wauchope: " Very good."

Another report: " Three officers of such-and-such a company have been killed. Captain So-and-so and Lieutenants So-and-so and So-and-so."

Major Wauchope: " Very good."

I saw much of this officer later. He was a born

fighter, a man of military genius. It thrilled me to hear his " Very good," calm and soldierly, concealing intense grief at the loss of brother officers. Useless to regret them then. One had to carry on, and he did with noble self-control.

It was a great lesson for us Territorials, lying there in the dug-out with brains on fire, and every muscle aching. Perhaps we in our turn must be killed. Very good.

Would the agony of that battle and the maniacal gnashing of the shells never cease? We of the 4th Black Watch, or at any rate those of my company, were strained, not to breaking point, but to the state of sleep-walkers. We went on, worn out, stumbling over dead men's rifles, ducking at a bullet's whizz, crouching for a shell, but still struggling forward with ammunition for the regulars in front of us. Our sense of the passing of time had been knocked out of gear.

Sometimes as we drew close to the fighting front line we exposed ourselves to German riflemen, and here and there men fell wounded, but we went on, staggering through the mud and slime and by the dead.

There was no battle joy in our hearts, but we would not fail our comrades of the 2nd Black Watch, or those poor Indians who were so baffled under bombardments, or the Leicesters, who had given us their spare food as they filed out of a trench to make a charge by sectional rushes.

Little memories come back as I write this. I think how sometimes the German rifles and machine-guns were too strong for us, and we had

to crawl on hands and knees through mud to avoid
them, dragging boxes of Maxim ammunition with
us. But we went on.

There was a moment when, ducking to avoid a
telephone-wire, I came a breath-catching crash. I
had slipped on a patch of half-dried blood. Strange
how slippery it was! My tired brain made a note
of it in words. "Avoid those pools of blood.
They're sticky and treacherous."

There were many wounded men picking a toilsome way over the wilderness of battle. There
was a Leicester in high glee. His arm was slightly
wounded. "Good old Jock," he said as he passed
me, and he smiled a greeting as if we were old
friends meeting at home. "Well done, Tiger,"
said I, calling him by the deserved nickname of
his regiment. "How's it going up there?"

"Pure murder," he said. "We shall be lucky
if we hold what we've got, but the Jocks have put
up a great fight. The Indians, too, but they've
lost an awful lot of their officers."

Then up and on with our ammunition, while
the Tiger went back, happy with thoughts of
Blighty (the name for Britain, that we had taken
from the Indians).

Our section kept pretty well together.
Nicholson, Joe Lee, and I were rarely parted.
Our platoon officer, a young accountant, Barney
Sturrock, and our company commander, Captain
Boase, appeared from time to time, primed with
news and orders. We did not like them to go away.
We were desperately afraid that in the confusion of
that wilderness our section might be forgotten, and

we might still be toiling to and fro through a desolation of exploding shells when we were entitled to a rest. Our section went on and on. Then Mr. Sturrock passed the order to collect all our men to go back for a rest. Night had come, and we moved to one of the new support trenches. We lay down in mud, huddled as close as we could for warmth. This and other new trenches had been got ready just before the battle in order that we could move to them for shelter if the Germans battered our known trenches too hard. Our main shelter here was the fact that the Germans did not know the trench was there. It was little more than a scraping in the mud and a bit of stockade.

Then Mr. Sturrock brought the great news that we were to get back to safety, to be "in reserve". It seemed a long time before we were actually moving off. As we were ready to go the Germans began a rapid fire, and we lay down for it to finish, just as you might step into a shop doorway to wait for a shower to pass.

We were to go to what I believe was the last line of redoubts (small temporary field-works). These could not have been more than a mile or two away, but we were so exhausted that it seemed hours before we got there. Whenever we halted and turned to look back we could see flares going up over the battle-line and shells flashing.

It was still dark when we got to the redoubt. Ah, what a fine, cheering military word that seemed on the march! Nick and I, staggering on, tested each other to see if we knew what a redoubt was. The word suggested some sort of

Crimean fortification. We comforted ourselves
with the thought that there would perhaps be
rough beds to lie on, a chance to burn a fire in a
brazier, perhaps even candles.

Hot drinks seemed then to be life's richest
blessing. At this time we had not the system
of company cooking which prevailed through
most of the War. A man went into the trenches
carrying so much tea, and sugar, and water, and if
he got the chance he made tea for himself with
any wood he could collect, or, if he had it, with
what was called a Tommy's cooker, the principle
of which was to burn solid methylated spirits. That
could only be done if you had some enclosed space
in which to hide your fire. There were many
moments of heartbreak when perhaps, after infinite
trouble in collecting wood and finding a place
where we could conceal our fire, and we were just
getting water to boil, an order came to move at
once to the right in file.

Whenever we halted on the way to the redoubt
men fell asleep by the roadside. When we had
roused them they were so heavy-limbed that it was
impossible to keep them marching well. Men
kicked the heels of those in front, and those near
the end had almost to run to keep up with those
in the front. What would we not have given to
have had the strains of the pipes to keep us going?
The pipers had sterner work to do then, acting as
stretcher-bearers.

At last the officer called to us to halt. " This
is the redoubt," he said. " The platoon will take
a right twist, and line the first trench they come

to. There must be no lights, and nobody must be out of the trench when day breaks, or else the Germans will shell us to bits. Rations won't be here till the morning."

Our hearts raged against this last appalling blow. Nick was for scouring the district to buy food at some farm. At this stage of the War civilians still occupied their homes close to the firing-line, and a man could sometimes slip out of a support-trench and come back in an hour with eggs to boil with our tea.

But even as we argued we were falling off to sleep. The thing we needed above all was rest. One or two of us got down in a very gingerly and experimental way into the trench. It was deep, hardly as wide as a grave, and contained a few inches of water. Some of us were for lying on the ground. "You can't do that," said a sergeant. "You know jolly well we shall all be asleep at daybreak, and the first Jerry plane that comes over will see us and turn the artillery on. Look at the fairground "—he pointed towards the front line— " see how close we are to the devils."

A cheerful voice broke in. This was C. S. McCririck, a man of noble character, whom I never saw out of humour with things. His light hair and spectacled eyes appeared just above the trench. "There's not much water in this part" he said. "We could dig a sump-pit lower down where it's deeper, shove our equipments down here, and lie on top of them, and then we shall be all right."

It was good advice. Soon McCririck, who was

very strong, lay down on his equipment, and another man lay, half on top of him and half against him. Nick and I decided to lie together. There was just room for this if we lay on our sides. We must have been asleep in a few seconds. Sometimes I half woke, hearing a man calling out in terror in his dreams, but I was soon asleep again. No guards were posted.

When I woke, Joe Lee, who never required much sleep, was sketching us. " Lazarus Rising from the Dead, new version," he said. He was quite cheerful. Some of our men were walking about in the open. The battle must have gone well. We were able to light all the fires we needed for our breakfasts. Then we got water from a ditch and shaved. The sky was blue, and it was much warmer.

Nick and I were eager to tell the people at home the stirring times the battalion had had. I drew out my little note-book to jot down incidents that came back to me, and to my dismay found almost all that I had written so far was illegible. Sweat or trench water had soaked the paper.

We decided to write a long letter to the *Dundee Advertiser,* as from one correspondent, written in part by Nick and in part by myself. We had hardly made a start when the alarm was sounded. We were ordered to man the stockades of the redoubt in order to repel the enemy if he broke through.

It was only a precautionary measure. The battle was still two or three miles away. After a while better news came, and we moved back to rough billets in battered houses. It was very cheering to see our commanding officer, Colonel Harry Walker, a slim brisk figure of a man, who you felt could be very severe, but was quick to note good work.

At night we took rations up to the 2nd Black Watch, who were holding trenches. We had then to bring back some of the Maxim ammunition we had taken up before with such labour. We gathered from this that the battle was broken off. It had not been the brilliant success for which we had hoped, but we were far from clear what had happened, and suspended judgement.

Then we went to rest in ruined billets in Richebourg. Though the Germans shelled us vigorously, we were too tired to notice it much. We were still contemptuous of their shells once we were in well-sandbagged buildings.

Word came at night that we were to move back for a real rest. We rejoiced—all but Nick. He was too weak and feverish to move. I reported this in dismay to Captain Boase. He was very kind, and gave Nick an opium pill. Then he said I might stay with my friend, and was to follow the company as soon as he was able to walk, or was taken charge of by the R.A.M.C. I was given the name of the hamlet for which we were bound. It was blissful just to lie for an hour or two longer.

Seaforths had come up, and they were exceedingly good to us waifs from the Black Watch. I think they must have been 4th Seaforths, Territorials. One of them, a teacher, with the beautiful clear articulation of the true Highlander,

shared with us a parcel he had just got from home.
We had cakes as well as tea, and Nicholson had
Oxo.

After a while Nick determined to make the
journey. Another of our men, a private who had
swollen feet, decided to trudge along with us for
part of the way, since there was no transport for
him. He could not get on his boots, and we
bandaged his feet and then tied puttees round
them. So off we went, arm in arm, hurrying away
from the shelled village. Once out of danger it
was a slow business, crippled as my companions
were, to make our way along the road. Fresh
troops were marching up. Many wounded were
straggling down towards casualty clearing-stations.
There was a shortage of stretchers, and we saw
doors being pulled down to carry the worst cases.
I kept Nicholson safely on the move, but had to
hand the other man over to the R.A.M.C. His
was a bad case of trench feet, and he could not
hope to march with the company. I heard a little
later that he had been sent to hospital at Dublin,
where he died.

Nick and I found the battalion at La Couture,
where it had halted for four hours on the road.
Indians who were resting near, seeing our men
hungry, gave them dates, and started to cook rough
cakes for them. Few of the Indians had any
words of English except swear words, and none of
the Black Watch had more than about six words
of Hindustani. But there was no need for phrases
to express the Indians' joy in helping us and ours
in the kind thought of our Indian comrades.

We of the Black Watch got on with these soldiers by sheer force of comradeship, unaided by any but the most rudimentary form of exchange of ideas. We had been warned at the beginning not to attempt to fraternize with Indians. We were told, officially, that they were queer fellows, and we could not hope to understand them. Moreover, we had heard, though not officially, the old story that the only way to make an Indian respect you was to treat him roughly. We never did that. As we passed Gurkhas, Sikhs, Jats and Punjabis we greeted them just as we did the Tigers of Leicester, or the Devil-may-cares of the Connaught Rangers. " Teek, Johnny," said we, " but Allyman no bon " (" Well done, Indian soldiers. The Germans are no good "). The Indians would reply : " Black Watch teek. Black Watch dam good." All would smile very happily.

Here let me record one of the stories in which my battalion came to take great pride. Pipe-Major Low was making a wooden cross when two Indians came to him with a piece of wood to put over the grave of a comrade. They showed that they wanted him to paint the wood and print on it the dead man's name. He did this, and after that they told all their comrades of the kindly pipe-major of the Black Watch.

Some months later Low was in hospital miles behind the line. Indian orderlies were on duty. On the morning after his arrival, the pipe-major felt something under his pillow. He found cakes and sweetmeats of the sort the Indians ate. By the bed was a glass of milk. Every morning he

E

found some dainty waiting. He was the only patient in the hospital who was so favoured. He could not at first understand it, but when he asked the Indian orderlies, they smiled. They had recognized an old friend of their firing-line days.

CHAPTER VI

CRUELTY TO CHILDREN

A FATHERLY job now came my way. I was given charge of a boy of fifteen or sixteen who had been with us in action, but now sobbed uncontrollably, and could not be quieted. Later we should have called it shell-shock. I had not seen the lad whilst we were in action, but I believe he had carried on well, and had spent most of his time at the side of our old battalion tailor, a big, elderly ex-regular, who, though a man of great heart and with the Regular spirit, ought to have been kept away from the fighting. No; perhaps I am wrong. I think he had been in the South African War. He knew what being under fire meant, and though he could not run, and puffed every yard of the way, he set a soldierly example. But he was done, this gallant old tailor, and I think after that he stayed at the quarter-master's stores at his tailoring.

The youngster, Private X, was a pathetic sight, his face swollen with crying. He had black hair, black eyebrows, and a round face which normally would be cheerful, and perhaps comic. It was now childish and frightened.

" Don't take me back to they shells, corporal," he said, again and again. " For God's sake get me out of this. I can't face they shells. I don't

mind they bullets, but I can't face they shells."
N.C.O.s had told him he must cheer up, or he
would be shot for cowardice, but this did not steel
his shattered nerves, nor did my reasoning with
him, and my attempt to cheer him with chocolate.

It seemed to me the best thing was to take him
to the medical officer and get a sedative. We had
many youngsters in the battalion, though, I believe,
none as young as X, and I was afraid his hysteria
might spread to others. So I reported the case to
Captain Boase, and he, failing likewise to make
any impression on the boy's terror, gave me permission to take him to the medical officer. This
was Major J. S. Y. Rogers, a name I cannot mention without feeling again the leadership and love
in his outstanding personality. He was a perfect
example of devotion to duty. He seemed to have
the priceless War gift of being able to do without
sleep, and when casualties were heavy brought to
his work a spirit of healing that made many forget
their pain. He was a brisk, hearty, and merciful
man, one we poor soldiers thanked God for. He
put a friendly hand on my shoulder when I went
into his aid post. " We're not going to have you
breaking down, are we?" he said. I smiled back.
" No; it's this boy I'm troubled about. He gave
a false age on joining, says he is only fifteen, and
he simply can't stand the shelling. What am I to
do with him, sir?"

At this X began crying again. Major Rogers
offered him a cigarette, and lighted it for him.

" Now look here, my boy," he said, in a kindly
voice. " I know you want your people at home

to be proud of you, don't you? You wouldn't
like your mother to think you were funking it?"

X admitted he wouldn't, but he said: "I can't
stand they shells. I don't mind they bullets, but
I can't stand they big shells."

"Oh, come," said the doctor, "you've seen how
the darkies stood it. You're a white man, you
know. You're not going to have it said that
darkies could stand the shelling and white men
couldn't."

But the poor lad had no spirit left. He must
have been knocked down or shaken by a big shell
exploding near him. I had to leave him at the first-
aid post, and I did not see him again. He may
have been sent to hospital, or perhaps he was given
some quiet job behind the lines, such as being
servant to a chaplain. He passes out of this story.

.   .   .   .   .

We were by no means sure how the battle of
Neuve Chapelle had gone. The official tendency
was to declare it a glorious victory, and to ridicule
our early hopes of sleeping in beds at Lille on the
night of the action. But we could see for ourselves
what a stern resistance the German had made, and
what losses had been inflicted upon us. Wounded
were tramping wearily from the front to the hospitals all the time. Some were being borne on
corrugated iron, torn from roofs. Everyone
admitted that our battalion had done remarkably
well in its first experience of fighting.

The 2nd Black Watch told us that some of our

men detached in the confusion of battle had charged with them. One of our companies had stormed a garrisoned house.

It was on the 14th, four days after the big bombardment, that we learnt from a French official message what had happened in the fighting. It was there related that we had carried the village of Neuve Chapelle, advanced both north-east and south-east of that village, captured one thousand prisoners and some machine-guns. The brevity and slightness of these claims, much below what we thought the British had done, came to us with a shock. It had not been so great a victory after all. A little later English papers came to hand, and we learnt that Neuve Chapelle had been the swiftest battle in the War. It was described as a wonderful triumph, but by this time we were sceptical of superlatives.

There were strange tales of the damage done by shells. Some of our men had gone into a German dug-out where five men were sitting in natural positions. Our men lunged at two of them with their bayonets before finding that they were all dead men. None showed any trace of wounding. Apparently they had been killed by the concussion of a big shell.

We could understand it, for some of the bigger explosions, even if you were ten or fifteen yards away, gave you a terrific shaking. You felt, as I noted at the time, that red hell had suddenly crashed into your consciousness, and a gigantic leaden fist caught you round the heart and thumped you in the middle of the stomach.

In another dug-out a card-party had been killed by a shell. One man, his head blown off, was just laying the ace of hearts on a rough blanket table.

.   .   .   .   .

We heard much discussion about the alleged shooting of prisoners. Before the action we had been told, though whether officially or not I cannot say, that if Black Watch men were captured, the Germans shot them. The story was, there was a sort of feud between our regiment and some of the regiments on the other side of the trenches. The Prussian Guards were said to have a special hatred of the Black Watch, and Crown Prince Rupprecht, who was in command over the way, was thought to be equally murderous towards us.

During the battle a British lance-corporal was said to have turned machine-gun fire on a mass of Germans who were surrendering without equipment, but a London officer protested and stopped the massacre.

You must remember that in battle, when some men have begun to surrender, there arise almost inevitably incidents of apparent treachery. Some men surrender. Others fight on. Each man sees very little of what is going on around him, for he may be lying crouched as low as possible in a shell-pit. A couple of men throw up their hands in token of surrender, and perhaps you rise up a little to beckon them nearer. At that moment other men, still fighting, and not having seen their comrades surrender, will turn their fire upon you. If then perhaps a comrade is shot dead at your side, you will be ready to believe in German treachery— or, of course, if you are on the other side, British treachery.

But I never knew of prisoners being murdered once they had passed through the hottest part of the battle. There were tales that some men would secrete a bomb in their pockets and then make them run until they were blown up. I can only say that I never heard anything like reasonable support—let alone evidence that would convince a court of law—for such stories. The probabilities are overwhelmingly against them. German prisoners were always ready, as it were, to work their passage and carry down wounded for us. I speak of what I saw.

CHAPTER VII

ON March 14th, a Sunday, the Bareilly Brigade was relieved and moved back to billets in and around Paradis, two and a half miles from Merville. My company was in the hamlet of La Couture. We were among civilians. It was Sunday, and a desire for thanksgiving took me to the local church. A British gun, firing from close by, shook down glass and bits of roof with every shot. The people were used to it, and no one moved an eyelid.

I met a friend there who told me afterwards of a grim duty that had befallen Lieutenant Gladstone's platoon. He had to take men to provide a covering party for engineers who were consolidating a captured trench. They had to creep out and form a long line round the workers. Some of the men were only a yard or two from the German trenches. They were on no account to open fire or expose their position. It was likely that German patrols would come their way, and their orders were to bayonet them as quietly as possible. All the time flares were going up, but the men worming down in the mud were not seen. Nor did any patrol approach. They came in after two and a half hours, stiff with cold. It seemed then a frightening experience, but we were all to have our turn of such duties.

We now had eight days' rest, but the word "rest" must be interpreted in a military sense. There was plenty of work to do, and the battalion was inspected by Lieutenant-General Sir James Willcocks and Lieutenant-General C. A. Anderson, both of whom praised us warmly. But how some of us hated those inspections! They were such cold and tedious jobs. We had to parade long before the General was due. We were tested again and again with orders. Our lines were dressed again and again. Then somebody would take it into his head that the platoon was six inches behind the line where it should be. We had to advance, then step back, then dress the line again. And so on.

. . . . . .

I never loved drill, but some of the men took a real pleasure in the rhythmical and mechanical handling of arms and in the unanimous clash and slap as we brought the rifle down or moved it to the shoulders. Presenting arms had a touch of poetry. I liked it once I could do it neatly. Fixing bayonets with a great flash and flourish of the blade always gave a thrill, especially if a whole battalion did it. But usually drill to me was pure boredom. I record this with regret. It would have been much better if I had taken it seriously. Captain Boase spoke to me about it sternly. " I want you to be a sergeant," he said. " I know I can trust you. I know the men like you, but you don't take hold of them as you should. You must cultivate a voice of command and make them do exactly what you want."

To be a sergeant: it pleased me mightily. It is a blood-warming word. I thought of Shakespeare's fell sergeant, death, strict in his arrest. And what was that other quotation about men going to death at the word of a sergeant?

Next day I was called out to drill the platoon. I could do the drill as a man in the ranks, but it had never been my ambition to be other than the man who obeyed. Captain Boase stood gloomily at my side. I felt as nervous as a man making his first after-dinner speech. For a time I was not too bad. The words, perhaps, were not quite right, but the men wanted to help me out. They knew the orders I ought to give, and moved smartly. Then, growing a little more confident, I decided to turn them about on the march. This is simple, except that you must so time the words as to get the men to turn together. If you are not careful some will turn at once and others wait for a step. Watching their feet, I shouted out boldly, "Right about turn." The boys did it perfectly, but there was a cry of anguish from the captain. He halted the platoon at once. "*Right* about turn!" he groaned. "That order was abolished years ago. Get back to the ranks."

Then I remembered "Right about turn" was the order we used to get from the old Crimean sergeant when we were doing physical exercises at school, but the word "right" had been cut out long ago, for a soldier always turns to the right and not

left. So vanished for a long while my chance of
a sergeant's stripes.

On reflection I was not sorry. I had no voice
of thunder. I never enjoyed ordering people
about, and it would have been awkward if I had
been a sergeant and my friend Nick had remained
a private. He, if anything, was worse at drill
than I was, and when given a chance did not so
much order the men's movements as make diffident
requests to them. He was a very gallant soldier,
all the same, like many privates.

.   .   .   .   .

As soon as Captain Boase's disappointment had
worn off, Nick and I decided to bite his ear for a
pass to Merville. Already we were speaking the
slang of the Front. If we wanted to get something from an officer we called it biting his ear.
If we wanted to tell a man we didn't believe him,
or had had enough of his society, we told him to
report himself to the colonel's horse. If an officer
was suspected to be on his way to us to make
trouble or find us some unnecessary work, we did
a flank movement, but if we suspected he was
bringing us good news or a gift of cigarettes we
were ready on the word "fix". If a man tried
to curry favour it was "pee-heeing". Anyone who
was killed "got the wooden cross". If a man was
said to have played the game it did not always
mean that he had played his part well. It might
mean just the opposite, that a man had tried to
achieve something by trickery.

Captain Boase readily gave us a pass on our explaining that we had heard there was a Norman Church at Merville in which we were deeply interested. We should have got the pass just the same if we had told him we wanted to go there for a good feed, but in the Army what is termed wangling gets into your blood : you are not content to make a reasonable request, but pitch your story as high as possible.

We liked Merville, then untouched by the enemy. The church was modern, but on the site of one burnt down by the Normans, and of later structures destroyed by the French and Huguenots. I felt a little homesick in the great market square. It was full of London buses, painted a slate grey and used for the food supply service. There were delightful canal vignettes.

A motorist went past. Something about the face seemed familiar. Yes—why, of course, it was the Prince of Wales. He had an air of boyish diffidence. We saw him once or twice later. Once he was interpreting for some men in a baker's shop.

·   ·   ·   ·   ·

A rich pleasure fell to us next day—a hot bath at Merville. Shallow tubs had been provided for us at a brewery, and there was continuous shouting just as at a boy's swimming bath, as we filled our tubs and pushed them about the flooded stone floor, two men in each. Snowflakes whirled through a broken skylight, but the water was really hot and

we were loth to get out and dry ourselves with our
shirts and hose tops. We stood about naked for
a time, searching our clothes for "Scots Greys",
for by now this regiment, which has made its
offensives in every war since the world began, lay
massed in every seam. We thought it occupied
our clothes in exceptional strength because we had
lain in billets where the Indians had been, and we
had seen these comrades pick "Scots Greys" off
their shirts, but owing to a religious scruple against
killing, place them on the ground, whence, in due
course (such was our theory), they attached themselves to us for rations.

We felt much happier now, talked no longer
about the battle, made friends with the French
people, and spent the evenings in the estaminets
and cottages where drinks were sold. At one of
these, two soldiers, father and son, met after they
had not seen each other for seven years. It was
one of the most cheering incidents I ever saw. The
father said when he left home his wife's last words
were: " Dinna come back without my lad."

           .   .   .   .   .

The church bells at Merville on Sunday morning
came to us like fairy music. In the afternoon,
being Church of England, I went to what the
Scots call an Isky-pisky (Episcopalian) service in a
little school-room, where water was boiling on a
stove while the service went on. An exercise for
17th October was still chalked on the blackboard.
Objects of natural history mingled with soldiers'

possessions. A portrait of Raymond Poincaré, looking very well-fed, beamed upon us from a laurelled border. The officers were on one side of the room and we men on the other. "Jesu, Lover of my Soul", and "Stand up, stand up for Jesus" were sung, the 23rd Psalm was read, the Creed was spoken, and there were prayers for the wounded and others.

A pay parade rejoiced us when we got back to billets. A private was given five francs. I, being a lance-corporal, got ten, and devoted part of it to having seven coffees for tea. It was bitterly cold and we had to break ice in a ditch before we could wash.

There was one piece of bad news that day. We had all been writing letters as fast as we could, and the officers, who had to censor them and see that we gave no information of military value, were overwhelmed by their task. Thereupon we were told that we must not write more than two letters a week in future. I obeyed, being a soldier, and made up for it by making the two letters very long. Sometimes they ran to four thousand or five thousand words, and they contained messages to my friends, which I knew my fiancée would copy out and despatch for me.

Many of these messages were to return thanks for gifts. My old colleagues in Dundee, having command of large circulations throughout Scotland, were able to draw upon an unceasing reservoir of goodwill for the benefit of soldiers. They sent to Nicholson, Joe Lee and myself big packages of sweetmeats and socks, knowing that we should distribute them as fairly as possible. It was pathetic to see what some of our chums were sent from their little homes. One poor woman spent her money on a tin of meat which was just like the bully of which we had such vast quantities that we found it used to make roads.

Whilst we were at rest we received severe and helpful training from the 2nd Black Watch. Major Wauchope was attached to us for this purpose. Men were picked to train as bombers, scouts, and snipers. Much better arrangements were made for the issuing of rations and for cooking in the trenches. In the future there was no need for each man to boil his tea. This was to be done when possible by platoon cooks. Later, we had a system whereby hot food was brought up in containers. Our shoes and spats were exchanged for boots and half-putties, and khaki bonnets were issued in place of the Glengarry.

Major Wauchope, dashing about on his charger and carrying a hog spear, believed in working us hard. We got very tired of this training—rest they called it—but it greatly improved the battalion.

.   .   .   .   .

It was Palm Sunday, 28th March, when we moved back to the trenches. Nick and I, with twenty others, were put in a communication trench, sixty yards from the German line, with orders to strengthen the parapet. Five men had been wounded at that spot the day before, and the

snipers still had their rifles set on it. We worked
with a will to build up the parapet. There was
a moment when I saw the flashes of two rifles
aimed at me at once. Extraordinary how marksmen could miss.

Our next job was to make a dug-out for
Lieutenant Sturrock. All the time we were working we were harassed by snipers in a house in
No Man's Land. We reported this to battalion
headquarters, and in the afternoon artillery opened
fire on the house and we had no more trouble.

Fights were going on in the sky, and one of us
was struck by a fragment from an anti-aircraft
shell. It cut open his right hand, but we patched
it up with our first-aid equipment.

An Indian came to us after a little while to tell
us of a Black Watch man who had been killed.
" He feenish—feenish," said the Indian, and held
his throat and made choking noises that sank away
to silence.

About this time came word of leave, magic,
heart-melting word. One of our men, Pal Stirton,
so called because he called every soldier "Pal",
was chosen to be the first to go, chiefly because he
was almost out of action with trench feet (swelling
due to the cold and wet). He walked nine miles
to Bethune, was there told leave was cancelled, and
had to walk back all the way.

He had no words to express his disappointment.
He was crushed. He felt sure he would not see
Scotland again. That was always our feeling
when leave was near. We had a superstitious
dread that we should be killed the night before

we left. I have known some of the best soldiers lose their nerve within an hour or two of going on leave. We did not ask them then to do any dangerous duty. We came to know too well how they felt.

CHAPTER VIII

THE GROWING STRAIN

THERE was a day when the cold seemed to get into our bones. The night had been frosty, but now it rained, the trench was muddy, and No Man's Land was grey with patches of mist. We had had no mail for a day or two, and our stock of comforts was low. We were not as a rule snappish in the trenches, but that day we were, having been working all night for several nights, and disturbed in the daytime by shelling.

I had to post sentries in two or three fire bays, and now and then go along to neighbouring N.C.O.'s to see that all was well. The mist all about made me a little fidgety. The enemy might be creeping up. One never knew.

I stopped to talk for a while with a private on my sentry rota, a man who had always a hungry, disconsolate look. In billets he had only one joke. He would suddenly call out " Tins outside," or some order like that. This puzzled me for a long time. I found it was what warders called out in a prison, and there was great laughter when some of them, pretending to be old gaol-birds, rushed to put their little food tins in line.

For the most part this soldier was morose. He never had any letters. He was that most pathetic creature, a friendless and unhappy man. Looking

up and down the trenches to see that no one was
near, he clutched my arm. " Corporal," he said,
" I've a present for ye." I thought he probably
had some souvenir to sell, but he pointed to a
warm cardigan under his tunic. " I'll give ye
this, corporal. It'll keep ye warm."

I would not take it. He needed it himself.

" Man," he said, " ye've been very good to me.
I'll never forget how ye shared your parcels. I
want you to see that I'll no forget."

I was touched by his gratitude, but fancied
something shifty in his eye. I told him when he
was on duty next, and went off to a neighbouring
fire bay. In due course I warned the would-be
giver of the cardigan for duty, and left him with
a periscope watching the shifting vapour in No
Man's Land.

A few shots were coming over from time to
time. They were probably fired from fixed rifles,
which had been set on suspected sentry posts in
our line and did not require a German to show
himself when firing. It was easy to fix them on
flashes seen at night time, and then fire from time
to time during the day.

Within an hour I heard cries of "Stretcher
bearer." I hurried along the fire bays to see what
the casualty was. My sentry had been shot in
the hand. A thumb hung by a shred of skin. He
was explaining to a sympathetic officer how he had
bobbed his head up to look at the creeping mist,
and at the same time was scratching his ear, when
a shot burnt his thumb like flame.

The officer was nervous. It looked as though

the enemy might be crossing No Man's Land in force, hidden in the rolling mist, with snipers active to keep our sentries down. We put two sentries at each post instead of one, and all N.C.O's were warned to be alert. Whilst these arrangements were being made, the wounded private was taken to a first-aid post, and later got home safely.

I felt sorry for the wretched fellow. Most of us had much to keep up our spirits—proud and affectionate letters from home, parcels every week, our faith in doing our duty, and living up to the ideals we had been taught at school, but he had no affectionate home, or pride of craftsmanship, or school sense of honour to keep him going.

I said nothing of the suspicions that rose in my mind that that shot thumb was a self-inflicted wound.

. . . . .

I often felt that I was not wholly a success as a lance-corporal. Rations had dwindled. The men of my section felt that the stronger personality their section commander possessed, the more food he would get for them. As I did not get them very much, they thought that I was too easily swindled by the sergeants. There was no truth in this, but hungry men grow suspicious.

We had a very bad system for distributing food. When the rations came to the company, the company-sergeant-major took what he considered his share. Then the sergeants had their go. Then the corporals. What was left was divided among the sections. It was not the system that a man would invent to ensure that all soldiers got equal shares.

A lusty lad called Hill was the chief mouthpiece of discontent. My own method was to divide the rations for my section, let the men take a share as they came up, and take the last share myself. That meant that if there was any difference between one share and another, I took the smallest.

Hill said to me, "Excuse me, corporal, did you have a poultry farm at home?"

"No," I said, "why?"

"Because you must be used to feeding chickens, not men. This lot wouldn't keep a full-grown hen alive."

I shared in the laughter, and thought no more about it, but Hill made a great story of it, and by-and-by the sergeant came up.

"What's this about the way you give out rations?" he said, with much warmth. "If I find you've been giving your friends more than others, I'll damned well have you smashed."

He seemed over-emphatic, and I told him so. In fact, we lost our tempers. I was never much of a fighting soldier, but no man can truthfully say that I ever failed to do my utmost to feed my men, and to feed them fairly.

There was an investigation. Hill produced a piece of bread I had given him as a twenty-four hours' ration. Nicholson produced the one I had given him. Mulligan produced his. I showed my own. Hill's was much smaller than the rest.

"It's the damnedest, dirtiest bit of work I ever

saw," said the sergeant. "I'll damned soon have that stripe off you," meaning that I should recede to the rank of private.

All but Hill at once took my part. "Don't you believe it, sergeant," they said. "The lance-corporal's as fair as fair could be, and he's always giving us food from his parcels. He's all right when he has it."

"That's got nothing to do with it," said the sergeant. "This man has not had his fair share of rations, and somebody's going to pay for it."

Thereupon Mulligan turned to Hill and said, "Come off it, you damned fool. Where did you put the other bit of bread you got?"

Thereupon Hill laughed impudently.

"Oh, yes," he said. "I forgot about that piece. I did a flank movement with it ready for my tea." And he brought it out from the pocket where he kept his pay-book and tooth-brush.

"Hill," said Mulligan, "you've got a face on you like a whinstone quarry."

The sergeant wanted to make a fuss about it, but, as Hill had owned up and the section went out of their way to tell me what a very fine fellow I was, I persuaded the sergeant to say no more about it.

Hill became one of my trustiest comrades, and he would volunteer to come with me if I was going out on patrol in No Man's Land.

. . . . .

As trench duty became more and more tedious,

and rations were scarce, the boys were often snappish, but malice never remained after a clash of
personality. We quarrelled less than men do in
a business office.

There was never the faintest trace of class feeling. Men showed very little interest in what their
comrades had been in peace time. I don't think
I ever knew what Mulligan was, or Hill, or any
of the men in my platoon, except one who was a
butcher, another who went about with a little
barrow selling paraffin, and, of course, the newspaper men. But the men rarely talked about old
days, and the works or the plough. Their thoughts
were of their wives and children and sweethearts.

Newspaper workers, as such, were not popular.
The Press then painted the soldier's life at the
Front in rosy colours. Our men would much have
preferred to be described as suffering heroes up to
the knees in blood.

If we grew a little boastful over our coffee in
some French cottage we never ranked ourselves at
this time with the Old Contemptibles, or the
Regulars who had come from India. The way
they carried on their trade and made no fuss about
it appealed immensely to our imagination. Our
admiration for the 2nd Black Watch was bound-
less. Merely to watch them loading up rations
for the trenches was a pleasure. Almost everything
was done at the double and with a minimum of
commands. Our men still shouted and argued
too much. You would often hear discussions
about it when we had a chance to sit at night

in some cottage, generally with a stone floor and papered windows, and a portrait of the absent husband in uniform on the mantelpiece.

We heard varied tales of the Germans from the cottage women. There was one, a woman of about thirty-five, with bulky figure, a monotonous tongue, and a bad squint, which her eyeglasses seemed to emphasize. She always wore the same slate-grey dress, soiled and torn, and her hair piled on top in a shifting mass, with tortoise-shell combs rammed in.

She bitterly denounced the Germans, and, raising her voice, would say, " Look what they did," and point to two broken chairs. But, as that was the sole damage inflicted upon her, we were not much impressed.

Our men did not get on too well with the French. They could not understand why the peasants grudged us water to drink and wash in. Local supplies were limited, and in the summer the French wanted the ditch-water for their own drinking and for the cattle, and they hated the sight some trench-soiled Jock stripping to the waist and washing at a wayside ditch.

I had to use all my diplomacy one night when one of our men, exasperated, spoke his mind to a French woman.

" *Allyman no bon*," he said.

The French woman agreed with much heartiness.

" Ay," said Jock with bitter emphasis, " and Frenchman *no bon*, either."

As the woman's husband was in the French artillery it was a bad thing to say.

.   .   .   .   .

One day General French came to review us. There was the usual tedious parade, the shifting and dressing of the lines, but we were not quite so resentful as usual towards all this ceremonial eye-wash, for we were keen to see the commander upon whose shoulders so historic a burden rested. Having seen many celebrities in my reporting days, I did not expect much : famous men are usually disappointing. French no doubt was a great soldier, but we could not expect him to show it in a speech. All the same, he made an excellent impression. He was, as we expected, a heavy, bowed, squat-shouldered man of the cavalry type, but what we were not prepared for was his exceedingly incisive way of rattling off a speech, a few phrases at a time.

Captain Boase asked me if it was possible to report this speech in the Dundee papers. There was no difficulty about that. In my reporting days I had practised memorizing speeches, without shorthand notes, and I was able to write out everything the General had said to us.

.   .   .   .   .

Then I had trouble with a private who became known as the Black Sheep of the Black Watch, but at this time he was just a black lamb, a merry, impudent fellow, with a bold eye for a girl. One day Private Lamb, as I will call him here, slacked persistently at his work of filling sandbags with earth. I had to crime him—that is, summon him before the company officer. He was unconcerned and relied on his wits to get him out of trouble.

After I had stated my case, Lamb put forward the defence that he had been misled by my manner. He did not understand that I had ordered him to do a piece of work. He thought I had merely requested him to do it as what he termed an oblige-ment to myself. This was a deadly counter-attack, for if an N.C.O. does not give an order as an order he is useless to maintain discipline.

To my astonishment, the officer told Private Lamb in icy terms that he was nothing but a common liar and that I had done my duty promptly in criming him for laziness and insolence.

The officer explained that he had been watching Private Lamb for some time, and on the occasion in question he was close at hand, but unobserved, ready to intervene if I did not make the party work. He had seen for himself that I treated the man fairly and efficiently.

This ought to have been a warning to Private Lamb. It would have been easy for him to reform, since in the Army, once you have done your punishment, it does not tell against you as in civil life. Thus no one thinks the worse of a N.C.O. who has been smashed, and if he behaves himself he soon gets back his stripes. But Private Lamb dramatized himself as one at war with the world,

one who did not get a chance, and he made up
his mind to dodge every duty he could.

For some time it was Captain Boase's custom
to call for volunteers for any dangerous work, such
as going on patrol in No Man's Land. The bun-
wallahs took it as a matter of course that they
should volunteer. In the early days Lamb also
volunteered at times, but now he refused to do more
than he must, and his black, mutinous expression
became habitual. I do not think this call for
volunteers for routine duty was a good system, and
ultimately it was dropped, because so many volunteers became casualties. Further, the system
encouraged men like Lamb to think that if they
used their wits they could always hang back in
safety.

Whilst in reserve or rest close to Richebourg
we had to go up every night to put up barbed
wire in No Man's Land or dig trenches. Lamb
got into the habit, as we were passing through the
last ruined hamlet, of asking permission to fall out
for a moment. This was quite usual, and permission was a formality. The N.C.O. would suppose
that Lamb, returning to the party, would join it
somewhere near the end of the line and would
think no more about it. If there were a hundred
of us working as fast as we could, perhaps with an
occasional shell or a stuttering from a machine-
gun to speed us on, nobody would notice a private's
absence. Lamb had realized this, and, having left
the ranks, he would go and hide in an empty shell
of a house, have a sleep, and then slip back into the
ranks when the party was returning.

I began to suspect this. I told Lamb I knew all about his dirty tricks, and if he dodged a working-party again I would have him up for it. He was frightened and appealed to me not to give a chum away. I am sorry now that I did not take my suspicions to the captain. Lamb would have received a severe punishment, but it might have been the saving of the wretched fellow. As it was, having only suspicion against him, having, too, a schoolboy's unwillingness to sneak, and thinking I had frightened him, I took no further action.

But Private Lamb was never again to be a good soldier. Dodging had got into his blood, and he knew all the tricks of it. If he had made proper use of all the craft he put into avoiding danger and work he would have been our best scout. I was very glad when he left us after reporting sick.

We heard from time to time of his career. Wherever he went he became known as the Black Sheep of the Black Watch. He returned to the Front with another battalion and repeated his wiles. Several times he just escaped being shot for cowardice, his officers being loath to have him bring greater disgrace upon the regiment. Ultimately there was nothing for it but to put him before a firing-party and shoot him against the wall.

He showed no fear when it came to the end, one grey dawn. During the night he wrote home to his people and acknowledged the justice of his sentence. When they took the lad out to his death, well drugged, they propped him on a chair. He asked for a cigarette. The rifles spoke, and justice was done. We, his old comrades, grieved much when word of this came to us. It was inevitable. It was what we had expected. But we could not think of Lamb as a wholly disgraceful coward. It seemed not so much cowardice as some criminal streak that made him live and die as he did. Who shall say that if he had gone into some severe regiment like the Scots Guards, and his first waywardness had been punished with ruthless justice, he might not have become as good a soldier as most? A strict battalion is by far the best. You cannot trifle with discipline in war-time.

CHAPTER IX

TIGHTENING UP OUR DISCIPLINE

WHILST we were at rest every effort was made by disciplinarians from the 2nd Black Watch to bring our battalion much nearer to the Regular standard of smartness. We were drilled almost incessantly. We had to begin again almost at the beginning. For half an hour at a time we had to do saluting, for there were complaints that our men, if an officer passed, did not spring to attention on the instant and salute with due deference. When the privates' day was done we N.C.O.s had to attend lectures. Their theme was always some aspect of the eternal problem of discipline. We must give an order as an order. We must see that it was instantly obeyed. There was far too much using of Christian names and nicknames by N.C.O.s towards the men under them. Men must shave first thing in the morning. Uniforms must be kept speckless. Above all, we must keep our rifles in first-class order, for, if not, they might jam in a moment of emergency that might mean our death. Old Sergeant Callary put this last point much better. " Pull your rifle through," he would say (he meant drawing an oily rag through it), " and your rifle will pull you through."

We were always glad to have our Commanding

Officer, Colonel Walker, at our billets, even though
he came to tell us the old, old story, for he had
a brisk, businesslike address and he made us feel
that to run the battalion on strict military lines
would be first-class business efficiency, as indeed it
would. His lectures to us made a big difference.
We began to realize in a way we never did at home
that on duty a soldier must subordinate everything
to the honour of the battalion. Even if he were
done some gross injustice he must serve faithfully
under the man who had wronged him. The
soldier was nothing; the battalion was everything.
We men might die. The battalion would carry
on. These were sobering and steadying thoughts,
but not stimulating.

Major Muir was lively to listen to. He was
sarcastic at the expense of young corporals who
thought a field-officer could teach them nothing.
To bring his points home to us he would emphasize
his slight nasal drawl. He fully exemplified the
old military maxim, "On parade, on parade, but
off parade, off parade", which means that whilst
an officer or N.C.O. may curse you and bustle
you about during drill, the moment it is over he
may be a man and a brother. Major Muir, in
spite of the rough edge to his tongue, was accessible
to any man in trouble. As we put it in our slang,
his was a juicy ear to bite.

To the Adjutant, Major Tarleton, fell the bulk
of the work of tightening up the battalion into
fighting efficiency. He was then, I think, our one
Regular officer. His way was to tell us bluntly
what we had to do. That was all about it. Since

he played schoolmaster to somewhat high-spirited boys it was not to be expected that he would be as popular as officers who showed all the easy-going generosities of civilian life. Once he reprimanded very severely a party who had failed to take up some sandbags to a certain point by a certain time. They had stopped on the way owing to a false rumour of gas. As there seemed to be thousands upon thousands of sandbags about everywhere, their leader did not think it worth while to risk lives for the sake of a few more sandbags. The men never forgot how Major Tarleton lectured them. Long afterwards the battalion would sing a parody, of which few of them knew the origin:

> " Oh I
> Don't want to die,
> I want to go home.
> Take me over the sea
> Where the Allyman can't see me.
> What is my life
> In all this strife?
> Sandbags is better than we."

There was nothing unkindly about this. The adjutant, of course, was absolutely right: everyone saw that. And we found he was a first-rate fighting man, efficient to the finger-tips, and we respected him to the utmost.

Sometimes we saw the results of inefficiency, and they taught us severe lessons. There was one blazing day when a ration party had failed to reach us during the night owing to heavy fire. We had nothing to drink, and the only pools within reach

G

were foul with shell debris or remains of the dead.
Most of us had never known before how painful
thirst could be. Some of us were so thirsty that
we rinsed our mouths with the foul water, after
putting in liver salts to purify it—if possible.

It was not easy to train the men's morals and
discipline all at once, but we looked with admiration and respect at the example of the Regulars
about us, especially of the 2nd Black Watch.

.   .   .   .   .

There came a day when I was put in charge of
a small detached guard at an important cross-roads
not far from Rouge Croix, that village famous for
its great crucifix, a grey figure on a slender wooden
cross painted red. It was used to support field-
telephone wires, which were slipped round the
upstretched arms and slung across to a spout at
an estaminet. The least reflective minds were
impressed by that great figure of Christ, bound
and entangled by the necessities of war, even as
were our own higher instincts, our hatred to shed
blood, our desire to love our neighbours as ourselves.

Twenty-four East Lancashires had been killed
outright by a shell at that spot at a rifle inspection.
It was believed that in some neighbouring cottage
a German agent could communicate deadly knowledge to the other side.

I marched my men to the scene of duty and
stood them to attention while I received the written
duties from the corporal of the guard whom I was

relieving. There was nothing complicated about the job. The chief thing was to guard all Government property in view of the post. We had no traffic-control duties.

In fact there seemed no particular reason why there should be a guard at that point at that stage of the War.

" You'll have a cushy time," the other corporal said. " If you want any coffee or bread you can get it at yon cottage down the road, but they won't give you *café rhum*." Off he marched with his little band. I posted the first sentry and moved into the kitchen of an empty house which formed our quarters. The only incident likely to cause any misgiving was a visit from some high officer. Accordingly I warned every man what to do if a high officer came, and I made sure that everybody knew the courtesies due to different ranks. I was pretty sure that the orderly officer of the battalion would pay us a surprise visit in the night and make sure that all was correct. But one of the men said this was not so; the adjutant would come, but nobody else.

Night wore on, and we enjoyed our separation from the company, with all its fatigues. I sat indoors reading a book.

The adjutant suddenly appeared with drawn revolver. His face was intensely grave and he signed to me to be silent. He had come in at the front door without my knowing and had found a man prowling about the attic. " He may be the spy we're after," said the adjutant. " He says he's one of our men. Come and see if you can identify

him." I seized my rifle and went upstairs to meet
the suspect. If there was going to be dirty work
I was ready to shoot first. But the man was only
one of my guards wandering about looking for
souvenirs. The adjutant was very disappointed.
" Keep your men under your eye the whole
time, corporal," he said sternly, and then
smiled.

Now and then the sentry came in to inquire
if the end of his turn was near. As it was
bitterly cold he would hang about near the
fire longer than I cared for. I began to realize
how slack we Territorials were. We were
ready to do our duty in the hour of danger, but
did not take seriously these routine tasks that
appeared of no importance. I was then so raw
that I was not certain whether I should allow
myself to go to sleep or not, but as I had had a
heavy day's work and was sure to have another
heavy day's work on the morrow, I thought I had
better wrap my great coat round me and lie down
by the fire for an hour or two. I lent my watch
to the sentry on duty, and he promised to wake
the next man at the proper time and hand the
watch on, each man rousing his successor. I fell
asleep and did not wake till after seven in the
morning. I went out to ask the sentry if all was
well, but there was no sentry. The whole guard
had been fast asleep. The moment I had begun
to dream, word was passed out to the sentry, and
he came in and all slept the rest of the night in
comfort and innocency. I kicked them awake,
and stormed, but it was no use to crime the men,

since I myself had gone to sleep and I was not sure that I had the right to do so. In a few months we were to be imbued with so different a spirit that such an incident would have been impossible.

CHAPTER X

THE SPIRIT OF YOUTH

O N the whole, these were toilsome but fairly cheerful days. We had the spirit of youth. We soon recovered from bad nights of shelling. The worst thing for me was the lack of sleep. The vermin on us grew so bad that we were kept awake even though we were dead tired after carrying wooden stakes up to the first line for three or four hours, or digging trenches. Somebody told us these "Scots Greys" could not stand cold, so one frosty night Nick and I took off our shirts and buried them until the morning, but this only seemed to make them livelier when we put the shirts on again.

Then I wrote home for a bottle of turpentine. Nick and I were ready for desperate measures. We covered our bodies, and especially the hair, with turpentine. Then we lay down, blissfully hopeful of long-denied rest. In a little while the skin was itching unbearably. The remedy was far worse than the disease. We did our utmost to take off the stuff, but we suffered as though we were being flayed alive. In the end we found the only way to go to sleep was to drink a tot of rum. So perished my teetotal resolution, killed by vermin.

The trenches improved rapidly with the drying

weather. We now began to garrison them on
our own instead of being intermingled with the
Regular battalion. The custom was for two companies to go into the line for three days with two
companies in support. The supporting companies
generally provided men for the working parties.
After three days they changed places with the
men in the front line. The stay in the trenches
varied in length in order to keep the Germans from
knowing when a change-over was due. Otherwise
they would have caught us on the move with shell-
fire, as, of course, they sometimes did. After six
to nine days a battalion would come out for a little
rest, and then the trench routine would start again.

It was often our lot to occupy old German dug-
outs, one for each man. They were a luxury after
the old days of battered and flooded trenches in
this district of Neuve Chapelle. The mails came
up regularly. We had all the parcels we wanted.
There was a happy day for me when a great box
of sweetmeats and other things, a gift from all the
Sheffield journalists, was brought to my dug-out.
It must have been four or five years since I had
worked in Yorkshire, and I was greatly heartened
by the kind thought of old comrades and old rivals.

When sunny days came our men began to think
more kindly of France. Hitherto they had considered it, climatically, a gigantic swindle. France
to them, before they came to it, was "sunny
France", the France of the Riviera posters, white
roads, azure seas and palm-shaded promenades.
The bleakness of Northern France, and even more
its waterlogged roads, destroyed cherished illusions.

Yet there were places and days of gentle delight. There was a farm with a willow-shaded little serpentine of green water at the back of an orchard. We lay there one afternoon, sunbathing our feet, wishing we could paint the hawthorn in blossom, and shouting words of cheer to many Indian wounded who were hobbling past. Curious how that golden afternoon comes back to me so clearly.

As a rule we just cried to Indians the few single words of Hindustani we understood. One night as we were on a carrying party we were given leave to fall out for five minutes' rest, and we dumped ourselves down by a native ration party. I said "Teek teek, Johnny," to the nearest man. He replied in English, quite good English, in level, velvety tones, with an aristocratic accent. I said, "You speak English very well." He replied, "I am glad you think so. I am a professor of English literature at a University." I wanted to ask his name and hear what he thought of the War, but the "Fall in" went imperiously, and I left the professor, never to meet him again.

Normally, if we were taking over a trench from Indians, our conversation would never get beyond this.

W.L.A.: "Rum rum, Johnny."

Indian: "Rum rum, teek. Black Watch."

W.L.A.: "Yes. Allymans—where?"

Indian: Yes—there.

W.L.A.: "Killed many—you—Allymans kill anybody feenish—many—yes?"

Indian: "No." (Pronounced with a very short "o."

Thereupon we assured ourselves we were in a quiet part of the line.

When in the front line we did not work hard during the day, but as a rule tried to improve our dug-outs. Private Mulligan (good luck to him, if he is still alive) a genial comrade from the country, with a very healthy red face, had become one of my little group of cronies. He was a fearless optimist, and used to cheer us all up by proving that the War could not last more than another month. He was always good company, and would amuse us with elaborate curses.

I fear we all used a few improper words to give expression to our feelings. It never struck me as a harmful habit. But some of the officers tried to keep it within bounds. One man used an improper adjective with regard to a staircase. An officer, overhearing, made him stand facing the staircase with orders not to move until he found his epithet had become accurate. When he had had a couple of hours of it, the man was glad to be released.

Mulligan knew all the sights and sounds of the fields. It was he who first made me listen to a melancholy wail flying over the trenches at night. I thought it must be some shell high up, but Mulligan said it was the cry of wild geese. The commonest wild objects of the landscape were strayed cats and strayed cattle. We came upon a pathetic notice on the door of an abandoned farm : " Please give the calves something to eat and drink."

The rats swarmed in all our trenches. Some

were a prodigious size. Once I was doing sentry
duty, and there appeared from the other side of the
parapet what looked like an old man's wizened
face. I drove at it with my bayonet, and realized
when I missed it that it was no German, but a
rat.

In the trenches we saw very little of the Germans.
By far the greatest part of our fire must have been
wasted. At night our patrols would bring word in
that Germans were out in front of their trenches,
putting up more wire. We would all fire in that
direction, but when you guess your aim like this
the results are very poor.

My first certain victim was a big man who was
coming down a communication trench. We could
see hurdles and rolls of wire bobbing along. Ordi-
narily that trench would have been safe enough,
but during the night our artillery had lowered the
enemy's parapet. I was told to watch the point
through a loophole, and fire if I got a chance to
hit a man. I waited a long time. Then came
a very careless party. They had evidently not been
warned to crouch at the danger point. I saw a
man who was taller than the others, and fired. An
officer watching at my side exclaimed: " You've
got him! By Jove! this isn't war—this is an execu-
tion." Sometimes at night, after we had fired at
the spot where we supposed a German working-
party to be, we heard the screams of their
wounded, but usually we had no idea what damage
we did.

CHAPTER XI

IN NO MAN'S LAND

I T was at night that we were most wakeful.
The brain-fever babble of the German
machine-guns went on spasmodically till
dawn.

Going into No Man's Land at night on patrol,
or to a listening-post, was much like the playing at
Indians of our boyhood. My first turn of it was
after we had had a lazy sunny day. Everything
was quiet. As dusk approached the sergeant
shouted to my dug-out: "That you, corporal?
You're for the listening-post to-night. Take Private
Mulligan and Private Robertson. Go out imme-
diately after stand-to." I answered: "Right ho,
sergeant," unconcernedly, but I could not help
remembering that Ralph Dick had been shot on his
first turn at a listening-post. The hour of "Stand-
to" wore away slowly. An officer came and
inspected our rifles. When it was dark the sergeant
passed along, calling softly: "Stand down."

I collected my two men, told the sentry I was
going out to the listening-post, and with a friendly
leg-up to the parapet we clambered over as fast as
we could. It would not do to be seen in the light
of a flare, for good German snipers missed few
good targets. We dropped into a slight depression, from which the earth for banking up the

parapet had been taken. In front we could see our lines of barbed wire twisting and intertwisting from post to post, with a tiny gap left in the entanglement. Through this we crawled. Then on, with nerves strained taut, on through the long grass steeped in night dew.

Crack! The report of a Mauser rifle startled our ears. That meant the bullet had missed by inches. Germans were a hundred yards from us— probably they had snipers out still nearer our lines. Crack!—Crack!—Crack!—Crack! came in a breathless stutter from a machine-gun. The bullets whistled and hit the parapet behind us with mighty thwacks. Had the Germans seen us? It looked a bit like it. We lay flat, holding our breath, and waited till that hideous stutter of death was over.

" Are you all right?" I whispered to the man behind. " Right as a pension, Linton," reported the stalwart Robertson.

We crept forward twenty yards to a hole torn by a shell. This was to be our listening-post till close on dawn. If we saw the Germans coming we had to warn our comrades, either by hastening back, or, if that could not be done, by firing on the enemy, but we had to use our rifles only in the last resort. Our main purpose was to use our eyes and ears, especially our ears, to detect any movement of the enemy. Crouching low in our shell-hole, we strained to pierce the gloom.

Mulligan caught my arm. " Is that a bloke in front?" he whispered. There was a dark, motionless shape a dozen yards ahead. We waited in tense expectancy to see the shadow move towards us. I gripped my rifle at the muzzle, ready to club the suspect. A flare went up. It revealed a post to which remnants of barbed wire, shattered by shells, still clung. Only that.

I soon realized how tricky the eyes could be for night work. I saw wooden posts move and bend. Once I fancied I heard them whispering in German, but Mulligan, who had the eyes of a gamekeeper, was sure they were only posts. There was no need to crawl out towards these mysteries. There were plenty of German star-shells to clear up the strange sights that loomed upon overstrained eyes.

Time lagged. It was very cold. We munched some chocolate. Robertson pulled at my sleeve. " There's a bloke at that old barbed wire up there," he whispered. I looked where he pointed, and saw a shadowy form. It moved. I was certain it was a man. " Keep well down," I whispered to Mulligan and Robertson. I moved forward with teeth set. I was deep in the grass, ready to spring.

" Who's that?" I whispered.

" All right, matey," whispered a hoarse voice. " I'm the Suffolks."

He was a scout of the neighbouring battalion to ours, returning from a lone patrol. He had seen nothing suspicious. He had been up to the German wire, and Jerry had no working-parties out. Back in our shell-hole I found the time passed wearily. There was no sign of a pending attack. A steady tap-tapping, as of mallets, came from behind the German line. Behind us we could hear the occasional shouting of our own battalion. A few bullets were coming over, but too high to catch us.

"Wish I was starting my furlough, corporal," muttered Robertson. "Shut up," said Mulligan, "it's not a furlough, but a wooden cross you'll get."

A pause, while our thoughts were busy with scenes of home. Ah, if only our dreams of loved ones would soon come true!

"The Allymans aren't singing to-night," whispered Mulligan. "Wonder what they're up to." But even as he spoke a rich baritone rang out from the enemy's trench, passionately declamatory. Perhaps he had sung in famous opera theatres. There was a haunting loveliness in his voice. But we had our ears to keep open for other sounds than Strauss and Wagner. The singing might have been a decoy or a stratagem. An ambush-party might be creeping behind us while we listened spell-bound to their accomplice.

After a while I could stand the tedium of crouching in this shell-hole no longer. I decided to press forward and see what could be seen. The grass rose knee high from the rough ground, and there was plenty of cover, but I must go slowly, lest I stumble into the midst of a German patrol. First I studied the look of things in order to get back safely and not wander by mistake into the German trench. It was a narrow span from us to them, but when you were crawling as low as possible, with the grass high above you, it was easy to lose your way.

Battles had been waged over this part of the ground since October, 1914. Many dead lay in the grass. I could smell them before I came to them. I crawled over thrown-off equipment, shell-torn caps and helmets, and great-coats, and countless clips of cartridges. Here was a German water-bottle of aluminium, a blue enamel one, riddled with bullets. Here was a broken Mauser, its mechanism red with rust. Two yards further, half-buried in the earth, was the curved blade of a Gurkha's kukri. But I was not here for souvenir-hunting.

I crept within twenty yards of the German firing trench. That was the limit of safety, for Jerry had cut the grass in front of his parapet to prevent the approach of our bombers. Soaring star-shells lighted up the scene, but flat in the long grass I was snugly out of sight of the sentries.

I could hear the Germans distinctly. Someone was calling out names in a sharp, authoritative manner. It was not a roll-call, but probably a sergeant giving out mails. Occasionally something jocular was said, and the men laughed. Yes; some sergeant would be giving out letters, and probably making jokes about those men who got letters from many girls at home.

They, too, no doubt, like some of our men, would pose as "lonely Tommy", and have a bevy of girls sending them letters and parcels.

I bitterly regretted that moment that I had not learnt German at school. What was the good of my Greek and Latin? There was no tapping of mallets to be heard now, but the ring of the spade and the bite of the pick came plainly from just behind the trench. This was nothing alarming. The men would be filling sandbags to strengthen their parapets and dug-outs against shell-fire.

Another German raised his voice in song. It sounded like a comic ditty, and the audience laughed heartily.

Then—my heart gave a jump. I could hear Germans approaching on their way back from patrolling No Man's Land. It suddenly occurred to me that the firing from the German trench had ceased some time ago. Doubtless Jerry's snipers had been warned to cease fire lest they should hit their own men returning. The Suffolk patrol had missed this lot. My nerves quivered. My heart thudded. But though I was nervous and excited, I was not as frightened as I should have expected. My own death seemed then, as in other moments of danger, a fantastically impossible thing. I wondered at this feeling a little.

The danger was over in a moment or two. Muffled footsteps passed about ten yards away. The patrol was making straight for a lane in the barbed wire. Once it was safe home I moved back speedily. Mulligan and Robertson were shivering when I got back to the listening-post. They were very bored. A little distance away a cat was yowling. Perhaps a flying splinter had wounded the poor creature. Robertson went in search of her, but she would not let him come near. She was a house cat gone wild, and living on the field-mice that haunted this desolate land.

" There's some poor blighter's wooden cross over

there all smashed up by shell-fire," said Robertson on his return.

One o'clock. It would not be long now before we returned to the cosiness of the trench. We gave ourselves up to anticipation of breakfast and then a long sleep. A shattering blast of machine-gun fire broke in on our thoughts. German star-shells shot up four or five at a time. No Man's Land was a blaze of limelight. We crouched down at the bottom of our pit.

The enemy was "getting the wind up". He thought our men were creeping over to attack him at the favourable hour of dawn, and was sweeping the approach with a hail of bullets. This went on for five, ten, fifteen minutes, and then tailed off into an occasional shot or two. The storm ended just as rainstorms end.

Now we could see the grass in front of us swaying against the sky. I could make out my companions' features plainly. It was high time we scurried back to report all well. With rising spirits we trailed our arms, and moved back, bending low. I shouted to a sentry who we were, and then we rushed over the parapet.

My first listening-patrol—the first of many—was safely over.

" Everything all right?" asked Mr. Sturrock, the officer on duty.

" Yes, sir," I replied, and I told him about the work the Germans had done and were doing in front and behind the trench. Then I went eagerly in search of mail, the perils and danger of the night out of my thoughts.

H

CHAPTER XII

THE BATTLE OF FESTUBERT

MY heavy eyes, struggling to open, fought the fight. My spirit, travelling back by painful ways from unimaginable remoteness, stirred my body out of its inertia. A girl's face, alight with tenderness, was looking down on me. I lay beside Nick, in the bewilderment of exhaustion.

"My brave Jocks," said the girl, "rest quiet. I bring you coffee—yes?"

With a smile she vanished. It was puzzling and dreamlike. I closed my eyes, sank back for a while, then, as cramp in my limbs asserted itself, made an effort to remember things. The memory of a bad time in the trenches—much shelling, casualties, legs and arms blown off, long anxiety as our reliefs came up, an interminable march, the discovery of the cart, the climb into its shelter from the wind.

"Nick," I called gently. The lad did not move. The girl came back with bowls of coffee, bread, and fried ham. She perched herself on the backboard, looking down on us maternally.

"*Camarade* no thirsty?" she said.

"*Camarade très fatigué*," I replied.

I called to him again. He woke with a nervous start, broad awake at once.

" *Mon ami, mon brave ami,*" I said, by way of introduction.

" Damn good breakfast," the girl pleasantly remarked to Nick, who rubbed his eyes gravely. She spoke soldiers' English, and there were inevitably swear words in it : profanation of such fresh pretty lips was inevitable. The sweet concern in her hazel eyes, the kindness in her face, were proof of a gentle nature.

" My poor boys, you fight—yes? Oh, I love the Jocks—dam nice, you Jocks. I bring more bread—yes?"

" Tell me your first name," I pressed her. She told me, but I could make out only the Christian name.

"Ah, well," she said, "call me Rosalie. The Crosbies called me that." (It sounded like Crosbies.)

" Who?" said I.

" The Crosbies," she repeated in surprise. " *No compris* Scotch regiment, Crosbies?"

" *Oh, compris,*" exclaimed Nick. " The K.O.S.B.'s."

That was it.

" What's this?" asked Nick, looking at our coverlet, a nice, warm carpet rug.

Rosalie laughed merrily. " I find you here at five this morning. I give you *couverture.*"

Bless the dear! We had fallen into good hands. A stainless sky shone festally. The warm air was good, but how utterly tired we were, our limbs racked with fatigue.

" I go now," said Rosalie. " Bring the mugs to the farm there, please, Jock."

" We'd better get up and see what's become of the old company," said Nick.

Slowly, for our Highland legs were stiff and painful, we got down out of our cart and looked around for the boys. The rest of them were wedged together in an evil-smelling huddle in a barn.

We gazed in at the men who lay still as the dead. Some rested with outflung arms; as if they had fallen in action. "Feyther's" legs lay across a sergeant's. Both snored grotesquely.

" Not thinking of waking, Willie?" I said to a chum. He woke with eyes of terror, as if caught sleeping at his post. Then he saw who I was, and went to sleep again.

Nick and I went to the farm kitchen. Rosalie was there, helping a large, placid mother.

" *Oh, la la!* " exclaimed the mother. " *C'est triste la guerre.* Many dead—yes?"

" *Oui, beaucoup, Madame,* " I said.

And that was about all Nick and I cared to tell her.

It was pleasant, just to sit there in the warm kitchen, where the brass and pewter shone, and the dinner on the stove smelled good. Rosalie went about her tasks with good humour.

" Mademoiselle Rosalie," said I, " you have been too good to us.

" Ah, no, Jock, that is impossible," she said. " One can be too bad, but too good—ah, no!"

.   .   .   .   .

It was the sunny afternoon of May 7th. Joe

Lee and I were talking to the old dame whilst she made coffee for us. I was making the little joke that I made with every Frenchwoman. I said I loved her good coffee (*bon café*), but I loved her good tea and goodness itself (*bonté*) even better. It sounded quite witty in French. The old wives always laughed.

In burst Nick, excited. " Boys," he said, " there's something big coming."

" Leave?" said I, with equal excitement.

" No," Nick replied, " another big biff. I've just heard the Quartermaster telling the R.Q.M.S. where to store packs."

This was decisive. Storing packs meant that we had to leave everything possible behind and get ready to move in battle order, the knapsack taking the place of the pack.

We went to our platoon's barn. Soon everybody was altering his equipment , and cramming his pockets with food. At 4 p.m. we paraded for inspection. It was impossible to quell the talking in the ranks. Everybody was making fun of everybody else.

" Silence," ordered the platoon wag. " Everybody will now stand to attention whilst Lance-Corporal Andrews and Private Nicholson shake hands and prepare to die." There was great laughter at this.

Emergency rations and field-dressings were handed out. Our blankets were handed in. We had all to display our primitive gas-masks, issued the day before. Men who had lost any article of equipment declared it. The company quartermaster-sergeant supplied their needs without question and without charge, though normally if a man lost anything he had to make it good out of his pay.

Nick, Joe Lee, and I had tea together in our cart. The mails had come up. We studied the Budget carefully, and wondered how the business of footing the War-bill would affect our future incomes, if any. We wanted to write home, but this was forbidden with the exception that we could send field post-cards, signing name and date only to certain stereotyped messages, such as "I have received your letter."

At six o'clock we were told to be ready at nine. A little before nine we were told that we were not going to move, and could lie down.

Rosalie lent Nick a carpet and a blanket for a bed. Both he and I stripped and slept luxuriously in our cart. We expected to hear the first crash of a bombardment at 4 a.m., but nobody heard it.

We were roused early, washed and shaved, and the boys collected flowers to put in their bonnets— "floors for ma grave," they said, laughing.

We were told that other battalions would take the German front line. Then we should go through and take the enemy's second line of trenches. We were told the artillery would blot out the German resistance just as it did at the beginning of the Battle of Neuve Chapelle.

All day we waited for further orders. Routine went on punctually. The drum-major brought up the mails. There were two big parcels from the office for the *Advertiser* men. As we already had our pockets crammed, we had a great feast, and were able to give something to everybody in the platoon. Nick, Joe Lee, and I had our tea in the farm kitchen, where Rosalie and her mother were. This was our menu:

Milk.
Chocolate Biscuits. Bread. Cake.
Spaghetti.
A piece of cold dumpling.
Figs and raisins.

Whilst we were disposing of all this, a sinister figure entered, head bound in bandages with great red stains, and eyes just peeping through. " *Ally-man no bon,*" said the poor soldier, striking a tragic attitude. The farmer's wife moaned: " *Oh, la la!*" but Rosalie burst into laughter. I thought she was hysterical, but the unfortunate man himself could not refrain from laughing. It was Tom Hutchison, who had bound up his head with field dressings and smeared them all over with damson jam. We were still uncertain whether we were to move that night. Little ration-bags were given us to tie on our equipment. I filled mine with figs, biscuits, chocolates and cheese. The waiting began to get on our nerves. We wanted the thing over. I put in my diary: " Shall be glad when we start. Don't like the idea of dying without ever seeing Gertie and Janet again. No philosophy can cure the yearning for one more sight of those I love. May God be very good to my darling and to my sister."

Remember this is not my own story alone : it is the story of many thousands of others. We did not go into battle like the brute beasts that perish, like sheep going to the slaughter, but in what might be our last hours thought very tenderly of those at home.

At eight o'clock came the time-honoured words, the order for which we had waited so impatiently : " By the right, quick march."

My company carried tools, the others ammunition. Many units were going up, and there was much traffic of ammunition and of guns. It was five hours before we reached our appointed position, an entrenched line where we were to await the bombardment.

We were somewhere near Festubert. Though at Neuve Chapelle we had had a very good idea of what we were after, here, coming to what to us was a fresh bit of the line, we had only vague ideas of the battle plan.

Once the sweat of carrying our rifles, spades, picks, and ammunition had dried on us, we began to feel bitterly cold, and were glad when we got an order to move into dug-outs. Six of us were put in one that was carpeted with straw. Sometimes we looked out and saw the stars shining. We listened for the noises of battle, but all was quiet except for the distant rumble of German carts on paved roads. It seemed that Jerry was bringing up rations as usual.

Chick Wallace, one of our best singers, was in our dug-out, and we got him to sing our favourite on such occasions. "There's a wee hoose". It made us think of our homes, and the old folk, and our sweethearts. It was only a music-hall song, but to us it was a hymn before battle. Chick was never to see his wee hoose again. He was blown to pieces an hour or two later.

At five o'clock a battery behind us started to hammer away, and in a moment or two there sprang up what seemed to be miles of British artillery fire. We looked out. It was a good day for the observers, the sky clean of any speck of cloud. The continuous shattering roar of our guns was varied now and then by the swish of German shells over our heads.

" Stretcher-bearer!"

The familiar cry went up, never to cease all day.

Wounded men were now walking back in our narrow trenches. English soldiers were pressing forward with ammunition. One had a football tied to his haversack.

At seven o'clock word passed along: " The German trench has been taken." We were very cheerful, everything considered. (This rumour proved to be untrue.)

We waited long past the time when we expected to move. This was ominous, for it meant that we were still a long way from the German second line, whatever had happened to the first. A sergeant put his head in at the dug-out. " Get your men out quick, corporal, and move forward as fast as you can. Force your way up. We mustn't be late on any account. Do not stop for the wounded. Get on."

It·took us some hours to make our way to a

position a little behind the front line. We were under heavy shrapnel almost all the way. At one point we had to rush across the open under fire. Whilst I was running my water-bottle broke loose, and I lost it, but I did not stop to pick it up.

The trenches were horribly jammed, and the cries of the wounded Seaforths and Gurkhas wanting to get past was piteous. But our orders were clear. We had to force ourselves forward. There was no stopping to exchange a friendly word with some poor cripple who wanted help.

Our bombers were in front of my section. A small shell—some called it a pip-squeak, a name not very familiar to us then—banged into the middle of them. Two of my friends, Jimmy Scott and Spark, were badly hurt, and Harley slightly.

We were getting far more fire than we expected. Jerry was surprising us. We never thought we should have anything like this trouble to get to the front line. We were all wedged together in the trenches, men of different units, bombers, riflemen, runners, wounded, and dying. We were so thick at some points that if a shell came we could not crouch down.

We of the Black Watch elbowed our way ruthlessly to the front. It was madness to stay there in that jammed trench, and be shelled to pieces.

When we came to the front line, or near it, there was more room, and we could lie at the bottom of the trench. Nick and I had kept together. A box of bombs had been left in our fire-bay. Nick pointed to it, laughing. I pushed it as far away from us as possible. There was nothing else to do but wait for orders.

I brought out my little note-book and scribbled a few words. This was part of my entry at 3.30 p.m.: "Under bombardment. Nerve-racking medley of roar and clatter. We are lying as low as possible. From the bottom of the trench I can see white puffs (shrapnel in the sky), also dense yellow-brown clouds where German high-explosive shells strike near our trench. Overhead aeroplanes are like filmy silver-grey moths against the glorious sky. Rushing winds accompany the whooshing and whooping and whistling of the shells, and earth continually topples over into the trenches. Have just been struck by a piece of shell—only a scratch on my right hand."

The bombardment continued for perhaps an hour. The German fire was vigorous and accurate. We were showered again and again by volcanoes of shell-torn earth. The call for stretcher-bearers never ceased.

About four o'clock we moved forward to a trench close to the firing-line, and were still vigorously shelled. There came a check. Men were bunching in front. Nick and I dropped to our knees for cover. Something struck the earthen wall hardly six inches from our faces and burst. Our faces were blackened, but we were not hurt. Nick said afterwards it was a rifle-grenade, yet a rifle-grenade bursting six inches away from our heads must have killed us. We argued about it later, but never came to a conclusion. It was one of those inexplicable escapes which came to every soldier.

We now saw why our progress had been checked. A narrow trench was crowded with dead, dying, and ammunition. Each of us had to take a box of ammunition and push on to the front trench. Here, too, we were shelled, though not as vigorously as before. Evidently Jerry knew all about our crammed communication trenches, and was sowing death where it would reap the biggest harvest.

We were still not wholly dispirited. We had still seen very little of the battle. Except for a brief dash, we had been in trenches the whole day, and had not seen one German. We did not know what had happened in front of us, except that obviously the German front line had not been taken.

We sat down on the fire-bay to wait. Our platoon-officer came and sat with Nick and myself.

" It looks bad," he said. " I don't believe our shrapnel's the slightest damned use for destroying trenches."

The bombardment had slackened, and we had a peep into No Man's Land. I shall never forget the sight. This is the note I made of it at the time:
" Ghastly spectacle of dead and wounded in a long line—'looking like sandbags', one man said. Our A Company had charged with the 4th Seaforths and lost heavily. They got ten yards from the parapet, and were mown down by machine-guns that burst out simultaneously. The Indians had gone over and had suffered the same fate. There was the

frightful smell of charred flesh from a casualty whose clothes had been set on fire by a shell."

A runner came along with messages. Mr. Sturrock went to report to another officer. He came back with a stoical face. " Sorry, boys," he said, " we go over next."

" Shall I tell the men?" I asked.

He replied : " No, not yet. They'll know soon enough. Just see they've got bayonets fixed ready."

Then he had another good look at No Man's Land.

" Not an earthly," he said, meaning there was no chance that we could reach the German front line. It did not appear to be battered by our fire. A soldier who had fought in South Africa came to me and said : " My God. They're lying out there on the wire like our fellows at Magersfontein."

We could hear the groans and curses of the wounded, and shouted to them that we would bring them in at dusk. An officer's servant, Private Smith, sprang over the parapet and went out to his master lying wounded, and stayed with him till the dark fell, but the rest of us were forbidden to try to succour our men. It was our job to go over next, and nothing else mattered.

The order came to get ready.

" I shall never see Forthill again," said Mr. Sturrock. That was the county ground where he had played cricket.

Nick said to me with affected self-pity : " Isn't it a shame that we're going to have a wonderful experience that we can't put into print? I could write such a grand article on how it feels to die young."

I was more practical. " Bags I that shell-pit in front where the two Seaforths are," said I.

At that moment a high officer came rushing up. He had only just been able to get through the press.

" My God!" he said. " Do you think you Terriers are going to succeed where regulars have failed?"

" Our orders are to go over," said Mr. Sturrock, quietly.

" Then for God's sake cancel them," said the other officer.

The word passed like a flash. There was no need to issue formal orders. We knew we were saved. Once again that day, by a million-to-one chance, we had been held back from death.

We now busied ourselves looking after the wounded in our trenches, and prepared to go over into No Man's Land as soon as dusk gave a chance to retrieve the poor fellows out there. Later our front quietened somewhat, but far off we could hear the artillery hammering away.

" I believe we've only done a feint," somebody said. " The big battle has been down south."

It was not for a long time that we learnt the truth. We *were* intended to break the enemy line. We had more guns in proportion to the front of attack than we had had at Neuve Chapelle, but the artillery work did not come up to expectations. There was not enough high-explosive shell to

destroy the fortresses the German trenches had now
become. Ammunition was largely defective, and
our guns had deteriorated through heavy use at
Ypres and Neuve Chapelle.

The first attack of the Indian Corps at 6 a.m. had
been a ghastly failure. The 1st Division on their
right had had no better luck.

A fresh attack was made, but was a complete
failure. There was a stream in No Man's Land
that was too deep to wade, and there were only a
few tiny bridges over it, some of them broken, and
others blocked with the bodies of those who had
been killed and wounded. The German machine-
gun fire that day had the easiest task to be
imagined.

Months later a friend gave me a souvenir, an
extract from the official dispatch on the action of
the Bareilly Brigade. This said:

> All three battalions pushed in part of their
> remaining companies following on the leading
> ones, but these men were knocked over
> directly they crossed their parapet. Each com-
> mander came to the same conclusion, that
> since our artillery bombardment was so inade-
> quate and the enemy's artillery, Maxim and
> rifle fire was in no way reduced, that it was
> useless and a waste of life to throw in the few
> remaining men left in their hands, and, there-
> fore, did not send their last reserve forward.
> This decision of theirs had my complete appro-
> val (the Brigadier's), and I decided not to send
> in the three companies of the 1/4 Black Watch

which formed my brigade reserve, for it was
evident that neither the enemy's parapet, per-
sonnel nor machine-gun had been seriously
weakened or reduced by our artillery.

Before it was dark enough to go over the top to
bring in wounded, my platoon was ordered to a
communication trench. By this time we were
greatly disheartened. The night turned cold. We
shivered in our trench. We could never lie down
for more than a minute at a time, owing to the
passage of the wounded. A man bandaged about
the knee and arm painfully carried on his back a
chum worse hit than himself. Almost every Black
Watch man passing up spread fresh news of
casualties to our friends. Our company commander, Captain Boase, was among the wounded.
When he got to the first-aid post he was obviously
in pain. Major Rogers said: " I'll give you
morphia."
 The captain said: " Have you got plenty?
Major Rogers replied: " Not too much."
 " Then keep it for the others," Captain Boase
said.
 We caught a glimpse of Colonel Harry Walker
and of the Adjutant, Major Tarleton. They were
brisk and energetic, and it put fresh heart into us to
see them. Colonel Walker, seeing some of the
youngsters who had come up in the last draft, and
had not been under fire before, said to them:
" Well, lads; you may have been boys yesterday.
You're men now—yes, men."
 We heard glorious accounts of the work of our

medical officer, Major Rogers, who never ceased for a moment to cope with his immense task.

Before dawn we moved off to the redoubts we had occupied the night before. We were disheartened at our failure to take any of the German trenches, and by the gloomy reports of the losses of our battalion. These were said to run to hundreds. We had never before had so grievous a day.

Nick and I were crammed together at a turn of the trench. We had lost our ration-bags in the congestion. I wrote in my diary : " Nothing to eat, nothing to do, will go to sleep. Men are saying battalion napoo-feenish."

The only cheerful news (though we did not all believe it) was that Italy had now come into the War, and had sent 150,000 men to take the Dardanelles, and that Holland was also in on our side.

In the morning I went to talk to some of the stretcher-bearers, and heard some heartrending stories of the wounded. One man, Masterton, misunderstanding an order, got over the parapet alone to charge, and going on bravely was killed. Some of our men dropped dead in the act of mounting the parapet. One of these was Lieutenant Weinberg, who had just shouted : " Come away the 4th." ("Come away" is Scots for "Come on".) There was a story of two of our men, dying in flames, and beyond reach, who went mad and fought each other.

The day was hot, and most of us slept. The Germans were a little nervy, and gave us shrapnel from time to time.

I

On the 12th we moved a little further back, where we could make tea in ruined houses. Newspapers had come up. We spent the day reading, writing letters, and searching our shirts and kilts. Owing, I suppose, to the heavy losses of our division, we were kept very close to the front line, instead of going back at once for re-equipment and a complete change. We did little but rest, though at night we had to sleep with full equipment, and one night, after we had been watching a German searchlight, flares, and flashing guns, we were suddenly moved back to close to the front line. It was rumoured that a native attack had again failed.

We had now plenty of food, made tea, and fried ham, and heard endless rumours about our future movements.

On the 17th rain began, and our redoubts soon became muddy and uncomfortable. We had not shaved since the 8th. It was now the 18th, and we looked like Crimean veterans. We had no chance to wash. Nicholson began to suffer from rheumatism. He was ordered to go to our transport to rest, but returned saying that he would be just as well with us as in their scanty accommodation.

Days passed. We were still in those muddy redoubts. Now and then bombardments sprang up. On the 22nd we moved forward to support trenches in the Orchard. The weather had brightened, but we were in a dreadful state of wild, muddy, and verminous dishevelment.

Happily we got our rations and mails without difficulty, although there was much shrapnel.

On the 24th Nick and I and the others of our

section, thanks to a large parcel from the office,
had chicken and tongue and pineapple for lunch.
It was not till the night of the 25th that we moved
back to billets, where we could wash and shave and
drink coffee with farmers' wives and daughters.

We had lost our jauntiness now. Men still
jested, but there was a more cynical turn to their
wit. One of the boys said: " The life's O.K. It's
the death I don't like." Private Robertson said,
quaintly: " Corporal, this War'll be the death of
me."

When we put up memorial crosses for those who
had fallen in the action of the 9th of May, there was
a sergeant-major who put a white cross on the grave
of his son, and a private who put a cross on the
grave of his father.

By now drafts of new men began to come up.
We veterans had often to leave our own sections.
Nick and I were offered promotion in other com-
panies, but preferred to stay with our old comrades.

CHAPTER XIII

JOYS AND SORROWS

WE were marching in the dappled sunshine of a road through a wood. Sleep-starved eyes brightened to the welcome of cool vistas. For a week we had stared at one shell-blasted field, with a lonely tree hanging its broken arms forlornly: a field lined at the other end with the most disagreeable people we ever met.

Now, as we marched in the sparkle of the morning, our spirits lifted. Snap sprang into the sergeant's " Right-left-right-left-pick up the step there in the blank file." The shuffling tread smartened. The lieutenant turned round from the head of the company with a rallying " Now, what about the band, Brough?" Whereupon the band passed its rifle to a neighbour, and proceeded to enliven the marching step and charm the sprites of the woodland (for all I know) with the strains of that classic lyre of Mars, the mouth-organ.

We sang. And how we sang! Like warriors. There was a merry lilt in the song. It expressed the self-respect of a fighting people's manhood. These were the words :

When WE go marching down the La Bassée Road
German loop-holes open wi-ide.
We can laugh and we can sing,
We can make the bullets ping,
*   Oh, we are the Cheery Jocks.*

The last line flung itself forth like a battle-cry:
" We are the Cheery Jocks."

We were dead-tired with the long strain of the
front line, the ceaseless digging behind the trench
in the blaze of sun, the ceaseless wiring and sapping
in front in the shell-riven night, the muscle-rack-
ing round of ration-parties, water-parties, cleaning
the trench, the sleep-shattering "Stand to". But
amid the leafy luxury of the little wood, with the
near prospect of rest—real, solid rest, with boots
and equipment off, and both eyes closed—our
hearts warmed.

On swung the company, grey with dust, kilts
which had not been off for a week drooping like an
auld wifie's petticoats, canteens clanking, rifle-slings
chafing the shoulders. A military policeman from
some brilliant non-combatant mob gazed at us with
the quiet, slope-eyed expression of a thoughtful
donkey. " My Gawd," we could almost overhear
him thinking, " why don't these Scotties keep
themselves clean in the trenches? Their buttons
is a disgrace."

His cold eyes stung us. " How would *you* like
to be a soldier?" shouted the Jocks. Virtuous in his
bright buttons, the policeman spurned us with a
glance.

And then came news—the Great News. At the
next cross-roads the advance billeting-party were
waiting for us. " Whaur's the billets?" we
inquired. " In the château," came the electrifying
news.

The château. It seemed like a dream. Dog-
kennels, hen-coops, stables: these were natural

enough; but a château, a wood-embowered, aristocratic château—it took our breath away.

" Nane o' your fancy French names for a clarty
bothy (mucky farm cottage), noo," said canny
Mulligan.

" It's an absolute fac'," was the reply. " A real
blooming old French château. It's a whacking
great place—twa ither Batts there tae."

" Och, ay," retorted Mac, " and a motor-caw tae
tak' us on parade and a bonnie lassie tae mak'
trench-pudding till us."

We marched under a grey archway and along
a winding drive to a massive many-windowed pile.
Our château fronted us with the dignity of its fine
old age. It bore itself with breeding. It was
steeped in the spirit of an olden time of chivalrous
men and dames. We cheery Jocks were not so
noisy as usual as we swung under another
crumbling archway into a courtyard with a space of
well-like coolness. For this was not quite the world
we knew.

Chalk marks on the doors showed where the
various sections were to sleep. " Dismiss," came
the order. Before you could have pressed a trigger
we were doubling to our rooms, and quarrelling
over the ownership of the best corners.

Eased of the burden of rifle, equipment, and
pack, and restored to the moral self-possession of
people with a week's holiday in front of them, we
began to luxuriate in the joy of living in a
château.

It was a quaintly rambling place inside. To get
to our bedrooms, sky-high, we had to go through

other bedrooms, opening straight into each other.
There were dark little corkscrew stairs of worn
stone, like those at Holyrood, trodden by so many
gallants of Scotland's historic and tumultuous past.
Here, as there, linger memories of the great days
done; days of be-ruffed courtiers and haughty
dames, of high-spirited oath and jested insult and
red-faced anger, and the never-ending tender service
of sweet-blooded women. We looked out from
high windows, now draped with nailed sacking,
on a widespread prospect of billowy-bosomed woodland under a singing sky. There were glimpses of
blue-clad peasants bent over their tasks in the fields,
and along a little grey ribbon of road in the gold-
and-green vesture of woods and fields the ceaseless
traffic of war went on, bringing food for the men
and food for the guns.

High were the times we had in our little cock-
loft. The only drawback was that the riven roof
yawned wide. When the rain came down with its
usual Flemish persistency it made us long for a wee
but and ben in auld Scotland. That was not our
only water trouble. Looking into the old biscuit-
tin in which our cook was about to boil water for
the tea, what did I behold but a dozen darting
minnows?

" Where on earth did you get the water?" I
asked. The cook smiled tolerantly. " Well, they're
a wee bit on the sma' side," he admitted, " but ye
canna expec' fresh saumon or boiled cod tae yer
tea at the front, laddie."

The château pump being out of action, whether
through old-age or an act of the King's enemies I

cannot say, the cook had filled his kettle at the nearest roadside ditch.

It was in trench-pudding that he excelled. With a few hard biscuits, the kind the Army calls buttons, after their shape, a handful of sugar, and a meagre spread of marmalade, he produced a delightful confection. " Ah, laddie," he used to say, " I learned that pudding in South Africa. Those were the days. A nigger used to drive up a few sheep, one would be given to so many men, and you had to kill it and cook it yourself, and make your own bread into the bargain. How would you have fared then, laddie?"

Not very well, I readily admit. This cosy old château, with pepper-pot turrets warming brown to the sun, was vastly more to my liking than the illimitable veldt. We settled in, and then, very very soon——

" We're going back to the line to-night," said a sergeant.

" Tell that to the colonel's horse," we jeered. But the sergeant was right.

.   .   .   .   .

My birthday fell on May 27th, when we were out resting. On the day before I received thirteen parcels, including one from journalists at Sheffield, with the most affectionate of letters from my friend of many years, R. R. Whittaker, now editor of the *Yorkshire Evening Post*. J. M. Hood, an old *Advertiser* man, and a quiet, thoughtful and stalwart comrade, shared with me a bottle-shaped dug-out against a house. Nick and Joe Lee had an arbour in the front garden. There had been a call for artists. Joe had stepped forward and found the job artists were wanted for was to paint wooden crosses. So now poor Joe was toiling while the rest of us made holiday with the parcels.

I read Dostoievsky's "Poor Folk", and delighted in its love story, though it seemed to me that it showed the inherent weakness of all novels in the form of letters: it was impossible to conceive of people living so near and seeing each other so often writing to each other so elaborately. I read, too, again and again, the Song of Solomon, my favourite reading all through the War, doubtless because I was young and in love, and could forget in its glorious passion present anxieties. I was twenty-nine, but still boyish.

It was very warm that day, with just a slight breeze, and thinking of those at home as I made notes in my diary, I remembered the old song:

> " *Oh gentle wind that bloweth south*
> *From whence my love repaireth,*
> *Convey a kiss from her dear mouth*
> *And tell me how she fareth.*"

Thinking of our future, I remembered another old song:

> " ' *I'll show you some other day,' quo' he,*
> ' *How we laugh and love in the North*
> *Countrie.*' "

You must not think that I, being a little literary, was different from the rest. Our ploughman soldiers, though perhaps they did not keep diaries or write poems, felt just the same emotions. All thought much of loved ones at home. They did not plunge into the orgies of vice depicted by some of the War writers. We should have been astounded if we could have foreseen the impression of sexual anarchy among us which was to be produced by novelists after the War. The general moral conduct of the men I knew was up to this time as good as it would have been at home.

Before we returned to the trenches I went to a Church of England service in a shed, where we sat on sacks of potatoes. It was a beautiful golden day. The tall poplars danced against a stainless sky. The chestnuts lifted up their white-and-pink candles, and the fruit-trees were in blossom. There was a scent of limes and of lilac. Laburnum-tresses delighted eyes that were tired of the khaki and mud colours of the trenches.

The troops were still in good heart in those days. There were plenty of jokes like that of the men who put up a dummy Kaiser by the roadside, and by pulling a string leading to a cottage made him salute as troops came up.

On June 1st we were given respirators of an improved pattern to guard against gas, of which we had had as yet no experience. We were very much afraid of it, for those early respirators did not inspire confience. We heard from old miners that the best thing to do was to soak a handkerchief in urine and hold it to the mouth if gas came. Better that than die of gas.

We went off to the trenches cheered, as usual, by a false rumour. This time Turkey was on the point of capitulating. We were never sure whether these rumours were officially inspired or not. If they were, they soon lost their value, for we learnt to distrust them. The Germans sometimes put up boards to tell us important news if they thought it would shake our confidence, and my impression is it was always true.

Some of their marksmen also put up boards. When a sniper had shot one of our men, he would hoist his score—for example, " 87, not out", or some other impressive figure. One of them claimed to have shot more than a hundred. We plastered his bit of line with every missile we could, and at night crept up and threw bombs where we thought he was lurking.

We now had a harder time in the trenches, having to dig night and day, and being frequently shelled.

I went out on patrol one night and was surprised at the number of dead lying in No Man's Land. I was not nearly as calm as I used to be. I could not be certain whether, say, the man lying so still by that shattered tree was alive or dead. My mate and I would wait a long time to see whether he moved. We could not be certain that he was not shamming dead before stabbing us.

By the time we had passed forty or fifty dead on our way to the German wire, I was ready to fire at the first field-mouse that squeaked, but we had

to hold ourselves in, for if we had revealed ourselves by a rifle flash, German snipers would have
been on us at once.

My orders were to go right up to the German
wire and find whether our artillery had made it
passable by our infantry. Further, there were
rumours that Jerry had a new engine of death that
was to be sprung upon us.

We reached the German wire in safety. It had
been only slightly damaged. A little to our right
we saw a ditch or sap. We crawled towards it
with extreme caution, expecting it to hold a
German listening-post. It was empty, and I
imagined it was a trap for our men if we advanced.
We should almost certainly bunch towards the
shelter of that trench, and then Jerry would open
on it with machine-guns. That was a useful bit
of information.

Now we listened to hear what Jerry was doing.
I could make out a steady "thump, thump,
thump". It went on unvaryingly. I asked my
chum if he could make out what it was. He
thought it was a pile-driver. I pulled out my watch
to make a note of the time. Then to my chagrin
I found the "thump—thump—thump" was the
ticking of my watch.

It was time to be getting back, for our careful
route among the dead had occupied an hour or
two. Then, to our anger, the British artillery
renewed fire on the barbed wire. A shell crashed
eight or nine yards beyond us, and the air buzzed
with spinning fragments of wire. We started to
race back, bending low. A shell-flash showed us

up. German rifles fired, and we jumped into a
new and still fuming shell-hole. Jerry fired a light
in our direction. With one impulse my chum and
I rushed for the ditch. Appalling blunder! Jerry
had a machine-gun set on it, and it started its mad
stuttering. We jumped out of the trench. Better
to risk the open and a star-shell near us than be
caught in that lane of death.

We got on as fast as we could, dropping now
and then into a shell-hole to get our breath. The
machine-gun was pouring lead down the ditch, and
bomb after bomb broke in. Our own artillery
were methodically pounding the wire. Jerry
undoubtedly thought we were a large party in No
Man's Land about to assault him, but the truth is
my friend and I were running from him like
frightened rabbits.

We got back all right, and the officer was pleased
with my description of how the ditch lay. I was
indignant that the artillery should fire while we
had patrols out. " Oh," said the officer, easily,
" I expect somebody forgot to tell them you were
there."

.   .   .   .   .

Whilst the weather was still hot we were lucky
enough to get far enough back to bathe in an old
boiler, but Nick and I were nearly knocked out
of the water by a shell, and had to run to cover
naked. Two civilians close by were struck by the
splinters.

Now rain came, and when on June 11th we

returned to the second line it was hard at every step to tug our boots out of the sticky slush. We had never known anything like this North French mud.

Moving back to La Couture, we found shelter in an Indian shack reared against the walls of a barn. I was put on guard over some promising apple-trees. A dead horse lay in the orchard, and I had to take charge of its burial. We had our unspeakable fill of burying our dead, and using blankets to collect the pieces of some poor fellows, but the burial of that stinking old horse stands out in my memory as one of the most dreadful jobs we ever had to do.

Nick, gentle, fastidious Nick, was one of the burial party, and when it was over he sat down and wrote a mock-heroic poem beginning:

" *Here lies a one-time faithful gee-gee,*
For a shell came and knocked him squeegee."

Thank God we could still laugh at our trials!

Shell-fire now came much farther back than before, and though we were comparatively safe, now and then a shell surprised us. Joe Lee, Nick, and I, scouting for coffee, suddenly heard one coming for us at a cross-roads. I fell flat on the road, but Joe and Nick stood still. The shell landed ten yards behind us, and by a great piece of good fortune did not explode.

All our men were not so fortunate, and there was a continual drain of casualties. Two or three would be wounded on a working-party. Men

would be killed by a pip-squeak in the front line.
Then perhaps there would be a couple of days
without a casualty. Then perhaps a couple of men
would be killed and three wounded while digging.
It was borne in upon us as morally certain that
sooner or later, if the War did not stop before long,
our time would come. It was out of the question
that we could escape some casualty. Our hope was
that we should get some nice flesh-wound that
would take a long time to heal, but leave us with
no disability after the War.

There was no dramatic collapse of the battalion
spirit. We still wanted to do our sworn duty, to
stand up like men to what we had come out here
for, but we went about it more gravely and without
bravado. We were becoming steady labourers and
tradesmen of war, just like the men of the 2nd
Black Watch when we first knew them round
Neuve Chapelle.

As drafts came out to replace casualties, we were
a little scornful of new officers with their eagerness
to advance. There was a youngster who, when our
trench was being assailed by whizz-bangs (so-called
because you heard a very silibant whizz before the
crash came), walked white-faced among us and
said: "Now boys, play up, and play the game."
An old N.C.O. said: "Excuse me, sir, this isn't
a cricket match. It's a bloody war."

We always got on well with the civilians in this
part of France. When we came out of the trenches
halfway through June, most of our men were playing football within half an hour of finishing a heavy
march after a fortnight in the trenches. Nick and

I went off to a cottage to drink coffee and see if they had any French papers. We found a happy pair of boys, Jules, fourteen, and Michael, five, and in a few moments we were having pick-a-back races. We contrived that little Michael's steed generally won.

We were inoculated for the second time. I was feverish and was off duty for forty-eight hours. It was significant that we were much slower this time in regaining our normal health. The War was telling on us. Yet even now it was not the intolerably tedious thing it became. Our leader, our inspirer, I might almost say our spiritual father, Captain Boase, was at home badly wounded, new officers had come, new N.C.O.s, but some of the old timers were with us still.

There was a night when Skerry, who had had a spell as officers'-mess sergeant, either came to pay us a visit or returned to duty with the company. He had a mandolin and gave us a concert that collected quite a crowd. He played Gounod's "Serenade", Elgar's "Salut d'Amour", and Jocelyn's "Berceuse". Moonlight showed our intent faces. The barn with misty white walls was outlined against a starry sky. The stately plumes of the poplars made a lovely pattern; near at hand the farm pond glimmered grey. We felt far away from war.

Then back to the front trenches. We had to work hard, for the trenches had been battered and required rebuilding and renewal of the wire entanglements. Days went by without an entry in my diary. One sentence supplies the key:

" Very weary through lack of sleep."

We were not wholly pleased at this amount of work we had to put into strengthening our trenches. They were now far stronger than in the early days of the War. We made them splinterproof. Plenty of pip-squeaks came over but did no harm. There was plenty of water in the trench wells. But the very completeness of those trenches was disquieting. We began to fear that we should never break through the German line. Our trenches were no longer temporary resting-places. Like the German trenches, they were becoming strongholds. If we had to perish, for God's sake let us perish soon and not go on year after year and then die miserably.

We were growing sick of it all, for every day seemed to make the work harder and bring new tribulations. We were now much troubled by mosquitoes, with their insistent, mechanical buzz. When would the War end? Some thought the Germans would collapse in another month. My impression was that we should call a draw to avoid European bankruptcy.

Nick, expressing thanks for parcels sent us by our colleagues at home, wrote:

I am not permitted to say much about the War in this note, but I think I may, without offence to the censor, say that things are very quiet and tense at present, and one sort of feels a big question mark overhanging the trenches: 'What's to happen?' . . . We Bank Street boys think much of you all at

K

the office and of the happy days we spent
there before this conflagration broke out.
The past and the future are all we can afford
to think about here. The less one contem-
plates the present, the better.

The truth was there hinted gently. No more
were the Scots papers to print the headline that
had become a standby: "Another cheery letter
from the 4th Black Watch."

Nick and I and many others talked of taking
our commissions. I believe he was offered one.
It would have meant going home for a course of
training, and perhaps when that was over the War
would be over. But we did not want to leave the
battalion yet. It would seem too much like giving
in.

The casualties increased—those casualties by
twos and threes, now and then, never at this time
in great numbers, but all the time bleeding away
our battalion.

CHAPTER XIV

DEATH OF MY FRIEND

THE War ended for Nick in the early morning of 13th July, 1915. We had been happy the day before. He and I had had a parcel from the office, probably the one for which he wrote the letter of thanks I have quoted. We had had encouraging letters from friends in Fleet Street. After our joint letter describing the battle of Neuve Chapelle, Lord Northcliffe himself had read it and, thinking it the work of one soldier, said : " This man can write. Take him on the staff when the War's over."

After that both of us wrote a little for the Northcliffe Press, but, of course, we always gave preference to our own papers at Dundee. Nick had had a message from Mr. Marlowe, the editor of the *Daily Mail*, and was elated, as well he might be, for he was certain of a great future if he survived. He could write a graphic description, and there was personality without egotism in everything he wrote. Here was a fastidious spirit hating war, but keeping steadily in view our great purpose.

When I last saw him alive he was finishing off the strengthening of a trench. A party had been filling sandbags with earth and had put them in position. Nick was not quite satisfied. He took a spade to weld them closer and climbed on the parapet. Perhaps a signal light showed behind him, or a shell flash. A German sniper, hidden in long grass, must have seen him clearly, and shot him close to the heart. Nick fell to his knees, crossing his hands, and died in a moment. Corporal Hutchison, a stretcher-bearer, climbed at once to his aid and was also shot.

I had left the party, its work virtually done, only a moment or two before to collect the mails from a ration-party. I had just gone into a dug-out, pulled down a blanket over the entrance, and lighted a candle to sort out the letters, when Joe Lee came and told me Nick was dead. I went with him. Hutchison was still alive, but died within an hour.

We lifted Nick into a sheltered place. He was very light, just a slim boy. There was much blood about his heart. It had smeared some of the letters in his pockets, but most of all it had stained a little luggage label with a jocular message from his sweetheart that he wore close to his heart.

Joe and I, as we saw that secret love-token, thought with heavy hearts of the poor girl in Scotland. What a symbol was here of this blind tragedy of the War! That little luggage label had been filled in with a jest, while eyes danced over it. Then, out here, it had cheered poor Nick. It had been a little secret he shared with only one. And now the blood of the heart it had warmed half-blotted out in death its friendly message.

In the pockets were letters Nick had been writing but had not finished. We took what was not soiled with blood to send home.

Then we had to go to our duties. Other hands

than ours carried Nick down from the trenches for burial.

We had seen much of death. Loved comrades had gone, but this was to me the most grievous blow of all. Nick and I had quarrelled at times, as soldiers under great stress will, but I loved that pure-spirited lad.

Physically, he was the weakest man in our platoon. He would often get a sort of trench fever. Joe or I would sometimes have to carry his rifle for him on the march, but he was very loth to accept help, and he made up for it. When volunteers were asked for to bring in wounded men from No Man's Land when German bombers were waiting for us, there was no keeping him back.

Captain Boase, his old company commander, wrote for publication this tribute:

" Like many of the battalion, he was to me not only a comrade-in-arms, but also a friend. To add to our sorrow, we have also lost Corporal Hutchison, who has truly died a hero's death. I have known young Nicholson to volunteer for a very dangerous bit of work and keep at it unflinchingly till finished, without, so to speak, turning a hair. I do not suggest there is anything exceptional in this (anyhow in the regiment to which he belonged), but it may please his friends to know that when there was special danger to be faced, Nicholson, like his comrades, acted up to the very best of the traditions of the Black Watch. Both he and Hutchison will be sorely missed."

Women called him "poor Nick" when he became a soldier, for it seemed so unlikely that this shy, slender lad could do a soldier's rough work. He hated the routine and the filth and the stenches, but he hardly knew in his anxiety to be brave what fear was. He was faithful to duty. He was chivalrous and steadfast in friendship.

Joe Lee and I had lost our dearest comrade. War, taking the best among us, now seemed to us a remorseless insanity. But he would not have had us think so. He fought in the spirit of a crusade. The men died: the battalion went on.

He was buried at St. Vaast Post. Joe and I were not allowed to leave the trenches to attend, but a company-sergeant-major and a brother of Corporal Hutchison were present.

Joe and I went to see the grave two days later. We found Nick lay near two apple trees, with Corporal Hutchison on his left. The artillery was booming close at hand as Joe Lee made a sketch of the grave for the old people at the manse at home in Dunfermline. Presently a body was brought for burial, a Warwick. None of his comrades could come, but a chaplain and four down-the-line men were there. The body, stiff and roped up, lay under a Union Jack on a stretcher. When the body was lowered into the grave the flag was taken off. The stretcher was laid on one side, and flies swarmed to lick the blood on it.

When we marched back for a rest the full force of my comrade's death came upon me. For almost a year we had marched side by side, shared our food

and our resting-places, shared our hopes. I was sick
at heart with loneliness now.

We were billeted in a silk mill at La Gorgue,
and now, for the first time since arriving in France,
I caught cold. Moreover, I was troubled by
festering mosquito bites in my ears, and the flesh
healed very slowly. How different I should have
felt if Nick had been there!

War's chief hardship for me was going for days
and nights on end with little sleep, for we were
doing hard physical labour nearly all the time. My
platoon was sent to garrison Duck's Bill—I think
that was the name, but I had no time now to post
up my diary. It was a ghastly, evil-smelling trench,
partly floored and walled with bodies. There were
many dead in front. Jerry's line was close and our
hold on the trench precarious. If men were killed
all we could do was to heave them over the sandbags to suffer what indignities they might. There
was a big German mine under us and we had a
counter-mine below it. The question was whether
Jerry would blow up our trench before we blew up
his mine. No one was allowed to sleep. You
might think that with the knowledge that we might
go sky high at any moment we should remain alert.
But we were so tired out that the wonder is the
whole platoon did not fall asleep.

Mr. Sturrock came along, found me nodding,
and had to shout hard before I answered. I went
with him to our sentry. He, poor fellow, was dead
asleep, and I kicked him awake, while Mr.
Sturrock tactfully looked away and pretended not
to notice.

We heard later that Jerry lighted his fuse first, and destroyed a garrison of Scots.

The scale of rations had now dwindled. A man was sometimes given only one slice of bread, a morsel of cheese, a spread of jam, and a pint of tea for a day, and we were greatly troubled by the shortage of pure water. We drank from the ditches and shell-holes, using liver salts to make the water palatable, but the ultimate result was consti-pation. I had not only deafness and mosquito bites, but also, in running through some barbed wire under shelling, I tore my knees and thighs, blood poisoning followed, and great boils made it almost impossible for me to walk. I was pressed to go to hospital, but did not want to leave the battalion, for going down the line meant that I should miss many parcels and letters; moreover, it might be that on recovery I should be posted to another battalion, or at any rate, another company. I went to the first-aid post, where Dicky Wood, who had come from a newspaper at Shanghai to serve in the Black Watch, was corporal. Major Rogers, hearing I was there, very kindly came and examined me himself. The upshot was that I was attached to the orderly-room to rest for a little while. Corporal Irons, our extremely able battalion clerk, was due to go on leave, and I was given his job for a few days. This meant staying in a French cottage with the battalion books and sharing the comforts of our staff men. The clerical work was light, and I spent most of my time playing with the landlady's children, Marguerite and Adelaide, who professed a great love for "le petit corporal," and wrote charmingly to my fiancée to tell her that I ate and slept all the day.

Going on from Laventie to La Gorgue, I spent some of my time in the interpreter's billet, talking to the mother of a little girl of twelve months, who sat on my knee and made happy noises. The husband was away at the front. " Is he wounded?" I asked. The poor woman replied, " Not yet." The child's grandmother showed me a little china image of the Virgin, brought untouched by so much as a speck of dust from a church shattered and set on fire by German shells.

When the men came in from the trenches, they looked woefully thin-faced. There was a story of a party who had fled when an N.C.O. cried nervously, " There's too much gassing." We were very much afraid of gas, then as always.

Now came a very jolly occasion : boxing competitions of the 2nd and 4th Black Watch. A bandstand in the centre of the market-place was used as a ring, with general service wagons as grand-stands. The finals on a Sunday were a great show. One fighter was tattooed from neck to foot. A picture of Christ being taken down from the Cross adorned his back, and a ship in full sail, baskets of fruit, and anchors decorated his front. Two Punjabis, who had never boxed before, were persuaded to fight by Captain Patrick. The rules were explained to them in their own tongue. They took off their yellow tassled turbans, and stripped their beautiful lithe bodies, which, unmarred by any spot, were a great contrast with the scarred and battered Highlanders. They shook hands, and bowed ceremoniously. Then started a terrific hitting out. They made little attempt to guard themselves. In the second round both were very frightened, but kept on grimly. Then one of them began to grasp the value of foot-work, and got in some fearful whacks before Captain N. Wilson declared him the winner on points. Our men roared with laughter and gave the two fighters a magnificent reception.

One night we had a concert in the market-place. My old comrade, Joe Lee, had by this time become famous for the poems he was writing at the front in the old Scots ballad form. To my mind no better war poetry was written, and I do not think Scotland will ever allow to die the memory of his two slim war books, "Ballads of Battle" and "Workaday Warriors", in which I have a tiny share of immortality as "Linton". Joe was now per-suaded to recite his poem, "The Mouth Organ," with musical effects by Private Brough.

Joe and I had always been warm friends, and now that poor Nick was gone we relied on each other even more. We dreaded the stuffy sourness of straw-strewn barns where dozens of lousy and unwashed men had to lie, and whenever possible we two slept out of doors, either wrapped in our raincoats and ground-sheets, or in a cart.

I wrote in my diary one day: " Must describe some day in detail the joy of sleeping in a farm cart; the last drowsy glimpses of stars, Joe's happy quotations, waking in the early morning with mist about the hedge-bottoms and along the fields, dew dripping from the trees; then sleep again to wake with the warm sun on the cheeks."

Towards the end of August we had bad days in the trenches. At one point we were very close to the German line, and much talk went on between us, always in English.

"We will give you whisky and cigarettes, Tommy," said a German. Our men replied with abuse. Then somebody more polite said, "When do you think the War will finish?"

A German replied: "When we enter London."

There was great laughter at this, from our side. At dawn several Prussians crept over to us and surrendered.

Lack of sleep remained my bugbear. "Awful night in dug-out," I wrote on September 2nd, "Joe and I sleeping in a bottle-necked entrance were continually disturbed by men who went out to their sentry-posts and came in from time to time. Slept on the fire-step in the afternoon, a mosquito net over my head."

The trenches became sloppy under rain, and we had only two hours' sleep in twenty-four.

CHAPTER XV

MY WAR WEDDING

BY this time I had every reason to expect early leave, as a good many of our men had already been home. My fiancée and I decided to get married. For one thing it seemed inevitable that I should become a casualty, and if I were lucky enough to get to hospital in Britain, it would be much easier, we thought, for a wife than a sweetheart to come and stay near me. War-weddings like this were still novel. I think mine was the first wedding in the Dundee district of a soldier from the front.

Word came that the Colonel wished to see me. I gave my buttons an extra polish and went off, wondering what was to do. He had heard of my coming marriage, gave it his formal approval as commanding officer, and best of all told me he would like me to return to the orderly-room staff for extra heavy work that was expected.

It was a heartening piece of news on the eve of my marriage, for it meant that for at any rate a little while I should have peace and rest. A staff job meant living in a much easier atmosphere. I was at once provided with a new kilt and apron. Dicky Wood gave me riding-breeches and a blanket, and I shared his sleeping quarters. It was exhilarating to sleep on a stretcher with kilt, tunic and boots off.

I took my meals with Regimental Sergt.-major Charles and Sergt. Irons, and we were waited on as if we were gentlemen by Private Linn, a Russian. The Sergeant-major was an old regular, with calm blue eyes, and a matter-of-fact acceptance of every danger. I had seen very little of him up to now, and he was killed a few days later, but I could well believe that he was a great strength to our battalion. I never heard him swear, or saw him get flurried, or snub any man. His one thought was duty, and he made all others think of it too.

There were three or four days of painful suspense till leave came. On the evening of 10th September I watch a German aeroplane, hit by a shell, turn over and over as it fell, while our men cheered. One of the airmen was killed, but his comrade was taken from the wreckage still alive. The next day I was up at 6 a.m. to clean my equipment and parade at 9 a.m. for leave. Willie Anderson and Pal Stirton were with the party. We walked to La Gorgue, then took train to Boulogne, through a level countryside steeped in drowsy sunshine. We could not get a train from London to Scotland on the Sunday, and we chafed bitterly at the waste of a day's leave.

I reached Wormit-on-Tay in time to see flowers being taken to the United Free Church for my wedding, and I met so many people whose sons, brothers, and sweethearts were in the battalion that it became a struggle to get to the church punctually.

We went for our honeymoon to Kirkmichael in Perthshire. It seemed a miracle to be in that lovely country, away from the war. We had three days there.

Then I had to begin the journey south. My wife came to London to see me off. I was again to be reminded that I was only a paltry lance-corporal. We travelled first-class. When we got to Edinburgh we had to change to another coach, and as I was talking to some of my friends on the platform a naval officer (the reader must here salute) and his wife got in. The officer called an attendant and told him that I could not be allowed to stay there. I thought this rotten, seeing that I had paid for my seats and got into the carriage before the officer, and I objected to my wife having to sit out in the corridor all the way to London. Just as the position was becoming strained an attendant came and said with friendly deference, " Is that your luggage, sir?" taking my rifle and pack. " Come this way, sir. Your sleeping berths are ready." One of my friends, seeing the trouble, had at once secured the berths. I am not certain that I showed an expression of Christian meekness as I left the naval officer (all salute, please).

CHAPTER XVI

25TH SEPTEMBER, 1915

I GOT back to find the battalion preparing for the Battle of Loos. The talk was chiefly of what gas would do. Just before the battalion was to move off I was given the confidential orders and maps to take round to the officers.

I was to see few of them again. Out of twenty officers who actually went into the attack, nineteen were killed or wounded. Among the killed was our beloved commander, Lieut.-Col. Harry Walker, who was, in the judgement of Dundee and of his men, the finest type of civic soldier. Of the men 420 went into action, and 230 were killed and wounded.

Only one of our officers returned unwounded from the battle near Manquissait on 25th September, and our casualties were so heavy that it was impossible to obtain a full detailed description. Most of my information came from my old comrade, Sergeant W. Addison, who is now editing a paper in South Africa. Our men's chief anxiety as they thought of the failure of 9th May was that our artillery would not prepare the ground sufficiently, but it was seen very quickly that there was now no need for anxiety on this score. There had been more than a week's slow bombardment of the German positions, with an intense bombardment for four days before the attack. Field guns had blown the enemy's barbed wire into the air, and the heavy guns had done serious damage to his trenches. Though the lines were 250 yards apart, pieces of German barbed wire, hit by one of our heavies, were actually blown into our front line.

The men left billets at Pont du Hem at 6 p.m. on the 24th, and entrenched between 8 and 9 o'clock. Some rain fell, but in the early morning it ceased. There was a puff or two of wind blowing towards the German lines, and it was decided to use gas in the attack. A British mine was exploded under the German front line at 5.45 a.m., and though half a mile away from the waiting Black Watch soldiers the quivering of the ground gave them a most uneasy sensation like that of an earthquake. Two minutes later all our guns opened on the enemy position, gas was turned on, and smoke candles began to issue great clouds of coloured smoke.

What with smoke, a thick mist on the ground, and enemy shells bursting on our front trench, the advance took place under confusing conditions. The adjutant, Major Tarleton, was hit whilst standing on the top of a parapet calling on the men to go forward.

Our companies moved steadily into the enemy's front line. Those Germans who survived surrendered in batches. Most of them were young, well-built men, pale compared with our weather-beaten veterans. As the Colonel and his staff were crossing to the German lines, Major Tosh was hit.

Sergt. Petrie began to carry him on his back towards our lines, but the officer was again hit by a piece of shell and mortally wounded.

As usual, our trenches were too narrow for the congested troops of battle, and Captain Duncan, standing on the top of the parapet in order to get his men along quicker, fell wounded with both legs broken.

Although it was still very misty and shells kept knocking out parties of our men, the Black Watch pressed forward at a good speed. The bombers searched dug-outs with bombs to prevent any lurking snipers being passed.

The 60th Punjabis were on the left, and the 2nd-8th Gurkhas on the right. Sometimes little groups of them would loom out of the mist and there would be moments of intense anxiety and hardly withheld fire until it turned out who they were.

The British guns now increased their range, and, though aeroplane observation was useless, did remarkably well. But the enemy was working with a clear brain, and he soon had a screen of shrapnel to separate our men from any supports coming up. Then followed the inevitable setbacks of a successful advance. Some men got too much to the left and were held up by the Moulin de Pietre, which was full of snipers doing deadly work from among the fallen bricks. Before they could be dealt with our troops were reorganized in a trench and some of them pulled out their pipes for a smoke.

The battalion had done even better on the right,

L

and here crossed four, if not five, lines of enemy
trench.   Colonel Walker, investigating the position, ordered Sergeant Addison to bring as many
men as he could find from the left to the right and
fortify a trench.   It was obvious that a counter-
attack would come, but it seemed possible to cope
with it.   Unfortunately our men had gone forward
so fast that some Germans had been missed.   Six
snipers firing at the back of our advanced companies picked off the officers one by one until only
Captain Air was left unhurt at this post.   The
officers were easy to pick off because they wore the
red hackle gleaming like a tropical flower in the
bonnet.   (Afterwards this honourable distinction of
the Black Watch was issued to all of us.)   Repeated
messages for reinforcements and ammunition were
sent back, and thirty men from the 2nd Black
Watch, that faithful Regular battalion, came up,
but much more help was needed.   The battered
ground, as one of the men put it, had been mashed
up like porridge, and many rifles became clogged
with mud and could not be used.   All our bombs
were finished.

The enemy then came on in great masses, and it
became necessary to retire.   Captain Air was
wounded in the retirement.   Meanwhile, Colonel
Walker, having realized the position, had to come
back himself to ask for reinforcements.   By this time
we had lost Battalion-Sergeant-Major Charles, that
quiet, elderly veteran who was as steady as a rock.
Private Watt, who was with him, went round one
side of a dug-out whilst the R.S.M. went the other
way.   A big shell burst, and when the rain of mud

had ceased Watt, going round to look for the Sergeant-Major, found not a trace of him. So perished as cool a man in danger as I ever knew.

As Colonel Walker was crossing the open he fell mortally wounded.

CHAPTER XVII

AFTER THE BATTLE

IT was now necessary for the whole line of our Brigade to retire, and at 11.30 a.m. the survivors of the battalion were back in the old front line, hard pressed by incessant shelling and rifle and machine-gun fire. Sergeant Addison, who had done great work that day, and was as clear-minded as he was brave, ended an account he wrote for the Battalion War Diary, with the stirring words: "It had been a grand advance, but at great cost. We had forced the enemy to turn on many of his heaviest pieces against us, and forced him to bring up very large reserves. Attacks were made at other parts of the line that day and the enemy's reserves had to be drawn off."

It had been a day of tragedy for the 4th Black Watch, but it showed that the old battalion could fight better than ever, and it was encouraging to find that our artillery, which we had often accused of killing our own men, had improved enormously.

I lost many good friends that day. My old colleague Skerry was last seen when our men were retiring. He turned back and charged into a group of Germans.

Pal Stirton, who had gone on leave with me, was one of the killed—dear old Stirton, who called every man "pal", and who, marching on the La Bassée Road, said, " If I'm killed, Linton, don't let them bury me by this road, for if they do I'll hear the Black Watch boys marching to the trenches, and I'll be sore at heart that I can't come with them." Dave Chapman was killed, too, a chivalrous, gentle soul.

Sergeant Irons and I, who had been kept out of the action, were now busy almost night and day with the business of verifying and reporting casualties and all the paper work of reorganizing the battalion. We were so short of men at the Front that although our battalion was no longer fit to fight, the survivors had to man the trenches well into October. Strong drafts came from home. The 2nd Battalion, those wonderful Regulars with whom we had been associated from the night when we first filed into a communication trench, had orders to leave France for Mesopotamia. My battalion now went to the 15th Division, and in a little while became part of the famous 51st (Highland) Division. Later we joined the 39th.

Early in December Lieut.-Col. G. A. McL. Sceales, 1st Argyll and Sutherland Highlanders, came to take over the command of the battalion, and to amalgamate it with the 5th Battalion, which had suffered severely like ourselves. We saw at once Colonel Sceales was a real soldier. He had not been with the battalion a day before every man knew it. His quiet efficiency was felt in every section, and under his leadership our poor battered old battalion was once more made fit to fight. He was big in every way, a little rugged, and deliberate in speech. He made sure of things. Above all, he was just.

We went right back to Allouagne, quite the trimmest village we had seen, with an air of comfort and solidity woefully lacking nearer the firing-line. Lieut. Pullan was now acting as adjutant, and came back from leave bringing a Remington Junior typewriter, which was a great help to the orderly-room staff.

CHAPTER XVIII

A BATTALION ORDERLY-ROOM

AT times we began to think that in the opinion of higher formations the paper war was more important than the flesh-and-blood war. We in the office worked from 7.30 a.m. till 9.30 p.m., and even so we did not seem able to satisfy the demands of our superiors for information.

When Christmas Day came we were so busy in the orderly-room that we forgot to cook our large plum-pudding, a gift from the Dundee public. But the mail came just before tea time, and we had a happy party at our billet. Our Robert the Devil, otherwise Private Watt, in civil life a cinema operator, but now cook to the orderly-room, flirted outrageously, to the amusement of all, with Marie Louise, aged fourteen. She showed her affection by telling him on every occasion that he was "no bon." She and her sisters showed us letters they had written to an uncle at the front, a man "très instruit," who had visited Buenos Ayres, Constantinople, and other cities.

There were five or six daughters, ranging from Julienne, aged 18, to Blanche, aged 7, and also a small boy of delicate appearance. Most of the girls were seamstresses, and made blue pantaloons to put on over the red trousers of the French infantry.

When it became known that we were to leave for
the Somme, Marie Louise became unwontedly
tender to Rober', allowing him to kiss her without
the usual "You no bon, Rober'."

Ah, Mademoiselle Marie Louise, in that village
of the Pas de Calais—do you remember little
Robert who was so fond of you, and was so soon
to die? He never forgot *you*.

As time went on, I became less eager to return
to my old section. In fact the old section had gone.
Most of the veterans—yes, we were veterans after
twelve months of France—had been given staff jobs
of some sort or another. Joe Lee, back from the
Bareilly Brigade, was officers' mess caterer. Willie
Anderson was with the signallers, and most of our
other Writer-Fighters had gone home for commissions. I hoped for one myself, but when Sergeant
Irons, the orderly-room sergeant, was promoted to
the 3rd Echelon at the Base, I took his place, and
for a time was content where I was.

A battalion orderly-room at the front achieved
dignity under difficulties. It might be housed in
a stable with half the roof off. It might be
crammed in a dug-out haunted by rats, where every
few minutes the crash of a battery shook out the
candle lights. Wherever it found shelter it
remained a centre of respect. The commanding
officer and adjutant here worked out their plans.
The regimental sergeant-major here read out
orders to his N.C.O.s; and here the adjutant's busy
clerks compiled the multitudinous records and
returns which were as essential to fighting as the
water-carts and gas-respirators.

Let us take a glance at a typical orderly-room while the clerks are bending over their makeshift desks. A row of dug-outs lies snugly tucked in against the embankment of a brown canal. We pick our way along the wired duck-boards laid in the mud, past the dug-outs of the commanding officer, the adjutant, and the mess. A little blue-and-white flag hangs limply over a tiny door that seems to lead into the embankment.

Stepping down into the dug-out, we find ourselves in a dim room walled and roofed with corrugated iron, supported by beams and rafters. A table of two candle-stained boards on ricketty trestles faces the door. That table, like many a veteran of the great War, is not much to look at, but what service it has seen! It was put together by the battalion joiner in scanty spells when he was not making wooden crosses. It has faithfully shared in the Odyssey of the battalion. It has been flung on a G.S. wagon and rattled away, with the boxes of records, on many an anxious move in the flashing night. It has been carried through trenches waist-deep in icy water and mud that pulled off the men's gum-boots. Clerks who wrote their casualty lists on it have long been written down themselves in casualty lists; but the battered table, survivor of shell-havoc and dug-out collapses, carries on.

The time is wearing on towards mid-day, when the commanding officer will preside over the disposal of business known as "Orderly-Room". The adjutant comes half-an-hour beforehand to see the correspondence, and puts aside any matters which, not being of a routine character, require the commanding officer's personal attention.

On the narrow duck-board path outside the dug-out, one or two officers and sergeants are collecting, spick and span as button-polish, dubbin, and clothes brushes can make them, in readiness for a commanding officer's parade. To come to "orderly-room" with hairy chin or dullish tunic buttons is a crime in the army code. The orderly sergeants for the week, one from each company, stand ready with pencil and detail book to take down orders.

" 'Tion!" thunders the sergeant-major to the parade. Arms drop smartly to the side, heels click, heads and chests strike the rigid attitude of drill-book diagrams. The commanding officer is coming. He returns the sergeant-major's salute, and with a "Stand at ease—Stand easy", the sergeant-major relaxes the taut figures.

The trial of prisoners begins. Each is marched bare-headed into the presence, listens to the concise evidence against him, says briefly what he has to say, and then receives his sentence in a word. To those accustomed to the leisurely methods of civilian courts the swift justice of an orderly-room is remarkable. There are no quibbles over technicalities, no ingenuities of argument, no flowers of rhetoric. Most of the charges are of drunkenness. "Sir," says a typical witness against Private Spud Ginger, " at 9.5 p.m. on the 1st I saw prisoner drunk. I confined him."

The prisoner rarely contests such evidence, supported as it always is by the word of the

commander of the guard to whom he was handed
over. It is useless to set up a fine-drawn distinction
between stages of intoxication. In the army a man
is either drunk or sober: there are no twilight
zones of doubt.

When a battalion was engaged in fighting, the
clerks had some share of the heat and burden of the
day. One of them might go up with the commanding officer and adjutant and remain with the
signallers and runners. If he had what might be
termed secretarial ability, he could be exceedingly
useful, for at times messages poured in, and an
intelligent orderly-room sergeant would spare his
adjutant the fatigue of being interrupted unneces-
sarily.

It seems incredible now, but it is a fact that
when, perhaps, a battalion had been fighting hard
for several days and the colonel, dead tired, was
having an hour's sleep whilst the adjutant perhaps
was visiting the company or reporting at the
brigade office, some frantic message would come
demanding to know the number of wire cutters the
battalion possessed. I never allowed the adjutant
or colonel to be wakened for a message like that,
but answered it myself. This was a violation of
military orders, but as my message was telephoned
as from the commander of the unit, no question
was raised about the sender.

Sometimes the adjutant or commanding officer
would be asked later, to his mystification, about
some message sent in his name, and once or twice
I get into some trouble because the commanding
officer did not know what the brigade people were

talking about. As our clerical work was the best
in the brigade and we did our utmost, there was
never any serious complaint. Even when once, in
making out some casualty returns, I killed the
wrong man and we had a stern letter from the
records office at the base, the adjutant merely said,
"Don't worry about that, sergeant. It's only Irons
(who now represented us at 3rd Echelon) pulling
your leg."

It is astounding that we made so few mistakes,
for you can imagine that in heavy fighting we, in
some dim dug-out at the back of the line, were
hard-pressed to check and verify reports, collate
them with villainously scribbled records from
casualty clearing stations, and with the help of
company quartermaster-sergeants sort out the kits
of dead, wounded, and sick, and send personal
effects to the base for transmission home.

When the battle was over, or rather when the
battalion was withdrawn from the line, the clerk
had to push on to the limit of the typewriter's
endurance.

The orderly-room was never allowed to stay in
one place long. When orders came to remove, the
books and typewriter were kept out as long as
possible, in case battalion orders had to be issued.
Then all the papers were gathered into boxes and
the long-suffering typewriter was swathed in
blankets to reduce the risk of damage. A party
of runners slid down the trench with the table, the
boxes, and the bundle on their shoulders, and at
length reached the dumping-point where carts
were waiting. Thence to wherever the battalion

was moving or as near that point as it was safe to take the transport, a G.S. wagon carried the orderly-room. Those G.S. wagons were as strong as rocks and as thunderous as galloping guns, but they were not made for carrying delicate typewriters. After every journey my lance-corporal would remark gloomily, "The old machine's got a shak. I doubt we shall have to get another." Then he tinkered at it an hour before it would work smoothly.

Perhaps it no longer printed figures on a level with letters; perhaps it skidded a space or two in every line, but it was a typewriter, even yet, and as we said, "Anything does at the front if it does."

Orderly-room work grew and grew. Although the regulations provided for a single clerk, at one time I had on my little staff one corporal, three lance-corporals, and Private Robert Watt, who did our cooking and cleaning. In addition, the colonel sometimes called in Lance-Corporal Anderson from the signallers to help with shorthand work, but this, as a rule, was my job, for I had never lost the shorthand speed I picked up as a junior reporter at Hull and Huddersfield.

Although by comparison with men doing the actual fighting we were enviably safe, we were by no means out of danger. Once, just when I had left the orderly-room, which was a hut in a wood, to go up to trench headquarters with the weekly returns for the brigade, a shell came and blew it to bits. When I got back next morning, my precious records were in tatters stuck on the branches of trees like a strange new blossoming.

Of that staff of six, I alone reached the end of the War unhurt. One went to hospital sick. All the others were killed or wounded, mostly in the last two years of the War when shell-fire had increased.

CHAPTER XIX

THE SOLEMN MAN

THOUGH I was now at battalion head-quarters, my colleagues and I were often hard pressed to find warm shelter. There was a strange night, somewhere near Philosophe, when all night long the wind was wailing like a banshee among the clustered telephone wires. It was more disturbing than the crashes of a neigh-bouring battery. We often slept through the booming of artillery, but this wailing of the wind and the gusts that swept into our doorless tumble-down billet kept us all awake—all save one of us, the self-styled "solemn man of the regiment," who snored beatifically in his nest of six blankets, four "smell-coats," and three or four scarves.

" Good Lor," said the corporal, who once upon a time was a callboy, " it's howling like an imita-tion wind in a drama."

Nature was indeed rivalling the theatre. The storm threatened to bring the house toppling over into final ruin. Fragments of the plaster that sagged from the ceiling laths kept falling on our beds. A loose end of one of the oat-bags nailed across the window slapped the woodwork viciously.

The cold was intense. One curled up to get the full benefit of the warm greatcoat outspread on the blankets, but sleep was not to be won so easily.

So we sat up and talked and smoked, and
pitied the fellows out on duty, trailing up flooded
trenches, stumbling and sliding and sprawling
with bags of mail or bread or coke on their backs,
or digging wearily into the curse-laden soil of
Flanders.

" It's somethink cruel," said an Englishman.

One thought of shivering sentries straining to
pierce the gloom, fighting back the sick hunger
for sleep, poor grotesque figures in tormenting
sheep-skins and gum-boots, thigh-high, grey with
the slavering mud.

The " solemn man of the regiment," who,
centuries ago—before the War began, in fact—
was an undertaker, and a good one, too, began to
talk in his sleep, a habit many men acquired in
the trenches. His words were slow and unctuous.

" Man that is born of a woman," he began,
" hath but a little while to live, and is full of
misery.

" . . . is full of misery." Our friend's voice
was impressive with the rising reflection of pulpit
emphasis.

" Only too bloomin' true," remarked the
Englishman.

The blustering, raving wind loudened. A great
piece of ceiling collapsed.

" Noo, that's enough, thrawin stanes at folk,"
cried a voice in mock anger. " Ye'll hae some o'
us doon the line in a minute!"

" Full of misery," drawled the sleeping man.

A furry coat went flying across the room. The
solemn man, his voice muffled beneath the smelly

garments, subsided into silence. But only for a while. Soon he was snoring again, slowly, with a certain funereal decorum.

Through the turbulence of the night came the dragging tread of a working-party returning from the trenches.

As they came nearer we heard snatches of music. Someone was playing a mouth-organ to hearten his comrades. And this was his message of good cheer in the dismal night: "Somewhere the sun is shining".

We still heard many talks of German snipers and spies behind our lines. There was the story of the devoted priest. He was the picture of priestly dignity. Tall, with sharp black eyes beneath bushy brows, a mouth of decision, and an air of command, he was a man you would look at twice if you passed him in the street. His cure of souls, you would have said, was the master-passion of his life.

The wreckage and filth of war soiled the once smiling village in which he laboured. Most of the people fled. Those who remained were under daily shell-fire from the Germans.

Misery showed in the hunted look, the pallor, the very walk, the clumsy, nervous walk, of these poor folk.

The priest stayed on. He was devoted to his work. Everyone said that. He went about all day long talking readily to any one he chanced to meet. The British soldiers knew him well. He spoke a quaint English, and loved to display it.

The slender spire of his church was fired on

M

twice a day. Our soldiers smiled at the shells going wide and killing a cow or a horse, or, perhaps, with a bit of luck, knocking out a brick or two. The priest did not smile, but he did not flinch. He was devoted to his work.

More and more of the villagers left their old homes. Before they drove off, with their household treasures on a rickety cart, they usually begged the good Father to leave for a place of safety as they were doing.

His stern yet likeable features would assume a wistful look. " Ah, no," he would say softly, " my duty is here. I do not fear the Germans. I must stay at my post of duty."

Without a doubt he was devoted to his work.

" Well, I'm a Protestant myself," said a kiltie, " but I must admit yon priest sets a good example."

The church became a more pathetic sight every day. Shells plumped into it squarely. They made havoc in the soldiers' billets. The little forest of plain deal crosses in the churchyard grew.

And now the spire was utterly shattered. The stained-glass windows became splinters in the mud. The shells tore open old tombs. Cold-blooded English soldiers peered in at the boxes.

M. le Curé still went about intent on his work. " I shall not leave my post," he said.

One morning they found him telegraphing to the enemy by a hidden apparatus in his cellar. He was shot.

He was devoted to his work.

CHAPTER XX

COMMISSIONS AND STAFF JOBS

THE question of taking a commission was one over which many of us brooded. It ranked in importance with the question: "How long will the War last?" For it was one of the few decisions over which we had some control. If a man was ordered to join a trench-mortar battery, he joined it, whether he wanted to or not, but he was not ordered to take a commission, at least, not at this time. No matter how bad things were, one always hoped that sooner or later one could get out of France for a rest by going home for a commission. This probably would mean being six months away from the fighting whilst one was being trained.

The men to whom this hope was denied, for educational reasons, had also their hopes of getting away from the worst of the fighting by being given staff jobs. Few men, even of the toughest and roughest kind, went on fighting year after year. Sooner or later, if they did not become casualties, many of them got jobs as camp-wardens or officers' servants behind the lines, or instructors at schools. Later, when I had become one of the few survivors of the original battalion, I was offered an appointment at the base, and the adjutant was good enough to say that I had earned it, but I did not want to leave the battalion after I had been with it so long. It was my ambition, when I could muster up enough pluck, to go back to a company instead of being a privileged headquarters man, to take a commission, and to end the War with my old battalion.

The spirit of the men was still excellent. That is to say, they did their duty very faithfully, but after the hard times they had gone through it was not expected that men would volunteer for dangerous duty as they used to do. Some of the old Territorials were becoming time-expired. The first I remember was Sergeant McLeod, our pipe-major, who, on being asked to re-engage for another term of service, did so at once, and was given a month's leave, but he was exceptional.

In March a batch of "time-exers" came into the orderly-room to be asked if they would re-engage. One or two said sheepishly they had not decided. The rest returned a sullen "No". Each was then asked: "I suppose you know there is conscription at home?" But that did not shake their attitude.

My impression at the time was that they were exempt from further service, but in any event the men preferred a brief spell at home, whatever might be the outcome, to staying on with the battalion. I could not blame them. They had, as they said, done their bit. It was time someone else had a turn. This was a general feeling. We had done our best, and as the months went on most of us had become battered and worn. My own trouble was impoverished blood and boils, and it was not till ten years later, after I had had two grave operations, that I became again the man I was. We of the original 1st/4th had taken our chance of being shelled and shot, but we knew now, after nearly a year in France, that our courage would not last indefinitely, and God forbid that we should return to civil life nervous, quivering wrecks for the rest of our days. We did not avoid our duty, but we did not seek danger: in the cant phrase of the day we had to watch our own interests.

After we had been six weeks away from the trenches and the routine of a rest-camp, with interminable working-parties, had begun to pall, we were moved to the Somme. It was then a quiet area, but we did not like the civilians nearly as much as we did the people of French Flanders. A schoolmistress came to me in great glee to tell me of a Zeppelin raid over Norfolk, Suffolk, Derbyshire, and Staffordshire.

She expected me to be pleased with the news, thinking it would help to rouse Britain from the inertia in which this land was slumbering, according to popular French opinion. I did not share that opinion, nor did my comrades. Then, as later, we were upheld by a feeling of spiritual oneness with the people of our own homes. Dundee was proud of us. There was no question of that. Other units were perhaps not so fortunate, but we were a city's own, Dundee's very own, and her first thoughts every day were for us. Even when news came of strikes among men doing essential war work, we did not rush to condemn them. Most of our men felt that their aim must be a good one, to prevent the exploitation of labour.

Nor did we think much of the Press agitation against the "Duds in High Places". We had seen much of Regular officers, and we believed in them. Our own Colonel, a Regular, was stern and unbending, for it was better so, but he was also just, efficient, and proud of the battalion. He may have seemed a little cold. I, who was much with him, know that he suffered intensely when he lost men, though he would have scorned to show it. Whenever we had had a bad time, he made suggestions to the brigade for avoiding future casualties. It was a great grief to him that he lost an adjutant, Lieutenant G. H. Scratton, most winning of all our officers. He was hardly more than a great, tall, light-hearted boy, with a gentle face ready to break into a smile. His voice was beautifully modulated, and with a slight English drawl. Though he never pored over the orders that flooded in upon us from higher authorities, a quick, absorbent mind enabled him to do his work extremely well. I have not the faintest idea who his people were, but I should say he was patrician to the finger-tips.

One day the battalion were leaving the trenches. Mr. Scratton preceded the colonel from a dug-out into the trench. A shell killed him at that instant. He had just made some farewell joke to the newcomers, and he was still smiling when dead. The colonel said to me the next day: " Very sad poor Scratton being killed, wasn't it?" Very rarely did he speak to me like that, as it were unofficially. It was the revealing of a heart that in wartime must hide its sorrows. The colonel knew the affection I was bound to have for this glorious young officer, and I knew what a wound this death tore in the colonel's heart. For a moment there was no difference of rank between us. We mourned our beloved friend. Then we resumed work. Men are killed: the battalion goes on.

But that sad day was still far off when our battalion left the Somme, not to return to it until the great battle had opened. We were ordered north to Renescure, near St. Omer, for the purpose of amalgamating with the 5th Battalion of the Black Watch. That journey will never be forgotten by any who took part in it, for it was bitterly cold, and in the last stage we had to battle with a blizzard.

CHAPTER XXI

BATTLING WITH A BLIZZARD

WE rose at 2 a.m., and at 4.30 moved off to Longeau, where we were to entrain. Cold and burdened, we marched without the usual singing, though away at the head of the battalion the pipers played. The dawn showed an empty, houseless landscape, almost like a Scottish moor. At the railway-station my lance-corporal (Norman Robertson) and I were in a van with sanitary men. It was too cold to keep the doors open, so there was a prospect of sitting in the dark for nine or ten hours. Then word was passed that I was wanted near the headquarters officers, and we were then put in a second-class carriage with Q.M.S. Dryden. Snow was falling when we moved off. All the way north there was storm and snow. We grew so used to the train that we were loath to leave it when, at 7.50 p.m., we drew into St. Omer station.

Glittering lamps troubled our sleepy eyes. For the fiftieth time since we had eagerly clambered aboard in the morning the long troop train jolted to a dead stop in the night. A lugubrious man with puckered eyes rubbed the frosted window. " Boys," he announced¡ without enthusiasm, " we've landed."

With the fumbling slowness of men prematurely

roused, we sought our packs and equipments, and cursed our chilled and stiffened limbs. The light of the platform lamps, thrown up by the snow, whitened our faces to a ghostly pallor. " Lord save us," said a Glasgow-Irish sergeant, " it's perishing cowld. God help the wounded who lie out to-night. The poor craytures will starve to death."

Shivering, we faced the night, to find one side of the train sheeted in snow. " Get those men out of the train at once," thundered a voice of command. The men in the closed vans were slumbering like the dead. Officers and sergeants from the second-class carriages rapped testily on the sliding-doors. Slowly the grumbling rank and file lumbered forth.

Orders ripped along. " Twenty men of the Duty Company to unload in front—hurry up." " Headquarters servants this way. What are you waiting there for?" " Fall in, C Company, in two lines facing the train."

Dull-witted confusion melted into military precision. Each went about his business. Horses and mules were run out of their boxes. Cookers and wagons clattered into line.

There came the welcome order to move. Out into town streets, where footfalls were a velvety murmur in the snow, on past massive piles, looming with a frown; on past a straggle of shuttered cottages to the gleaming countryside.

" How far is it, dae ye ken, Jock?" asked one.

" God knows," said his chum. " If it's far I'll fall out—I'm fairly done to begin with." After a

long march in the early morning and ten hours
cramped in the train, packs weighed grievously on
our shoulders. We stumbled and slipped on the
frozen road. It began to snow. There was a
whip-like edge to the wind. We prayed that it
would not be very far to billets.

" I wish we was in the trenches, Bill," somebody
said after an hour on the road. Many of us wished
it.

We could hardly distinguish ditches from road.
Men struggling dumbly on crashed into the ice.
Some fell out and lay in the snow. We N.C.O.s
had to rout them out and force them on, or they
would have died in the blizzard. To throw off my
pain and misery I forced myself into the past, and
at times, quoting scraps of Latin, believed myself
to be an ancient Roman soldier.

Sergeant Forsyth told me the whole of his
platoon, officer included, fell out, except himself
and three men. The officer gathered the stragglers
and gave them a hot supper at a farmhouse, where
they stayed all night.

We kept looking out for our village, and rejoiced
several times to see distant glimmerings, but they
turned out to be railway signal-lamps or motor-car
head-lights. When we got to the village we found
the billeting arrangements had gone wrong, and
had to find places wherever we could. Norman
Robertson and I went to a barn, and being without
our blankets, slept under straw among the rats.

In the morning I got water at a château, and
our Signals Officer, Lieutenant Currey, a South
African, showed me round the old hall, lofty, with

a ceiling of oak, plaques on the wall, pewter and bronze on the shelves, and a fine air of comfort.

We had about twenty punishment men in the battalion, and on the night march through the snow some of these were lost. The next morning a message came to the orderly-room from the prisoners reporting that they had formed a guard-room for themselves at a place two miles away, and could they please have their rations and mail sent to them?

.   .   .   .   .

We were by no means pleased at the prospect of amalgamation with the 5th. Our chief constable, Sergeant Watt, said he would be ashamed to be found dead in the 5th, but the alternative would have been to be split up into drafts for other Black Watch battalions—which we should have hated—and anyway we had no choice in the matter. Actually we of the 4th and 5th became very happy together, and made an exceedingly good battalion, known as the 4th/5th. We now formed part of the 118th Brigade, along with the 1st/6th Cheshires, the 1st/1st Cambs, and the 1st/1st Herts. By way of concession to our battalion pride, we were promised that whatever changes were made the 4th and 5th would go home after the War as two battalions, not one.

Being now far from the firing-line, we hoped for comfort, if not rest, but the billets were wretched. For orderly-room we had a stable without a window or stove, but an old woman at a

cottage close by became friendly, no doubt because
I spoke some French, and would interpret for her.
Once, to my consternation, she came into the
orderly-room, when prisoners were being tried, to
tell the colonel that she had a cup of hot coffee
waiting for me. Luckily the battalion sergeant-
major had no idea what she was saying, or he
might have died of apoplexy. I gently edged the
dear old lady away from the Presence with the most
rapid French at my command.

CHAPTER XXII

WE MEET THE AUSTRALIANS

QUICK moves followed, always a matter of concern to the orderly-room, for we had an enormous number of returns to furnish, and it was very difficult to keep up with them on the move, when most of our records were packed away in a cart. It was intensely cold, and an outbreak of scabies, a form of itch, came at a most unfortunate moment, for it meant that blankets were called in for disinfection, and we were left with only one per man.

On one of our moves towards Caudescure we came for the first time upon several hundreds of Australians and New Zealanders. Dare-devil experience was written in their faces. I thought many of them were of the bush-ranger type, with an easy play of muscle, and a fine horsey air. They had the names of their towns written on their slouch hats, such as "Oomalong". Their uniforms were a dusty grey-white. They walked along anyhow, hands in great-coat pockets, shoulder-straps undone, saluting nobody. They were sunburnt, and we heard they had come from Egypt, and some of them had fought at Gallipoli. A crowd of them raised a great cheer for the Black Watch. We could not respond, as we were marching at attention, but that cheer gave us immense delight. It

was the first we had had since we left Dundee so
long before.

We were now nearer the countryside we knew
so well, Pont du Hem and the rest, and we found
local people as kind as ever. I was billeted in the
loft of a house where two seamstresses lived. They
were very poor. One night as I was returning to
the billet the wind tore a rough newspaper that was
their only bedroom window, and I caught a
glimpse of the pair, sitting naked, side by side on
the bed, searching their vests for lice. On leaving,
Norman Robertson and I had to drink a little glass
of cognac to our safe return.

We had five months in this familiar area of
Festubert, Givenchy, and Richbourg St. Vaast.
The battalion's worst times were in the Givenchy
area, where they occupied a chain of posts in
swampy ground well in advance of the old British
line. Gas was much in our thoughts. On
May 27th, at about 8.30 a.m., I began to wonder
what on earth the pioneers had been doing with
their chloride of lime. They used this to deluge
the middens, and the smell now began to come into
the billets. But it was not chloride of lime. It
became strong enough to tarnish our polished
buttons, and we began to have headaches. We
found it was gas that had been liberated by the
Germans at Loos, eleven miles away. We also
had an experience of tear-gas, which we believed
was dropped in bombs by aeroplanes. After this
we had gas-alarm tests.

Though I got on very well with the French, they
had no great opinion of the English. Joe Lee told

me of a man who said to him, with comic emphasis : " *Soldat Anglais—confitures.*"

I had not now the time to make friendships I used to have. Night or day I could never be away from the orderly-room for more than a few minutes. Still, I liked the work. I had the honour to serve officers of noble military quality, like Captain J. Kennedy, the very best type of ranker, who had a mind for every detail. Seeing him, active, fearless, and encouraging, I thought of him as the best leader I had met for a forlorn hope. He left me pretty much to do the work of orderly-room sergeant in my own way. So did Mr. Scratton, who became adjutant in June, when Captain Kennedy was appointed to command the 13th Welch Regiment. I think the work was done well. We were very proud of the way we kept our records.

Whether these were kept well or ill made a great difference to the comfort of our men. There was always much correspondence on pay questions, and if records of a man's pay, allotments to family, punishment, promotion, leave, pay remittances to family, and so forth, had fallen into arrears, it might have robbed a man and his family of money they needed. We had great difficulty in keeping track of men in hospitals or on detached duty, but we did our utmost to let them get their mail regularly. Next to feeding them this was the most important thing to keep them in good heart.

Regulations about proficiency-pay had become a tangle. Men at home, being able to fire musketry courses and in other ways show their proficiency, were given supplementary pay. Our men, having been in France a long time, could not get any, not having qualified by the tests. But obviously they were proficient soldiers. I studied the regulations, and wrote a little paper on them, giving full instructions on how to claim the pay. The result was that most of our men obtained unexpected increases. This made me much more popular than any fighting I had ever done, and when later I left headquarters and went to a company the reception given to me was overwhelmingly friendly. I am very proud of this proficiency-pay episode. My friends say that I know nothing about finance. Don't I?

As midsummer approached, the battalion, under Lieutenant-Colonel Sceales, seemed to me to be better than ever before. Conditions had changed. Men fought differently now. The long quiet days in the trenches, when we were reasonably happy, had given way to ceaseless front-long battle with bombs, rifle grenades, and shells. Cutting-out raids, directed to the capture of prisoners, had become a vogue.

The ceaseless drain of casualties went on. One night I shared a bed in a hut with Sergeant D. Smith, of Carnoustie, and took a great liking to the man. I felt we should be great friends. The next day he was firing rifle-grenades, when the rifle burst, killing him. It was often like that. You would share a cake with a man at dinner-time, and be writing a letter of sympathy to his widow at tea-time.

CHAPTER XXIII

OFF TO THE SOMME

WHEN the battle of the Somme opened we were still among the reed-reflecting waters and poppied fields of Givenchy. For a time I shared a billet with men of a tunnelling company, miners from Wales, Scotland, Derbyshire, and Australia. They told me of one brave fellow who was in a mine which fell in. He could have got out, but went further in to help a wounded chum. Then a further fall occurred preventing escape. A hole was drilled through to him, and liquid food was sent down a pipe. Attempts were made to drag him out, and shifts worked unceasingly. After three days he could no longer speak through the pipe, and a further fall made it impossible to take him out. His mates opened a subscription fund for his widow and family.

We knew we should soon be going down to the Somme. There were the usual symptoms of excitement, premature orders, premature destruction of records, rumours that the move was postponed, cancelled, and advanced, and that the rest of the division, but not our battalion, were to be in it. Taking our rest whilst we could, we lay out in the fields, handkerchiefs over our faces to keep off the infernal flies. At night many of the men preferred to sleep in the open, because we were in the most rat-infested place I ever saw. Rats would jump on our faces when we were in bed, and in daylight we could see them moving about on the roof, picking a stealthy way among the broken tiles that burned red against a burning blue sky.

As we looked out on the flaming poppies and the vivid charlock, and, above all, on the bronzed wheat that was now within three weeks of harvest, we thought continually of that other harvest on the Somme.

We went to Le Touret on 9th August, a swelter-ing day, after saying good-bye to the remnants of two Yorkshire battalions that had lately come from the Somme, and told us that the battle was pure murder. Our packs were loaded on motor trans-port, but it did not cheer us to be relieved of the burden. We knew it meant a stiff march to come. Our marching strength was 38 officers, 845 other ranks.

For the most part going south we sweated and swore, but comic incidents would keep breaking in. There was a first-class row at one billet, because we started typewriting at 6 a.m. and woke up the landlady.

In some of the marches men fell out, but not a man of our company failed. Our company com-mander, Captain Donald, presented each of us with a packet of Three Castles cigarettes to show his pleasure at our sticking it.

. . . . .

Mercifully it was some days before the 4th/5th

Black Watch was ordered into battle. There was no mistaking the importance of this enormous struggle, for the roads were almost jammed with night traffic for many miles, and vast stores of shells lay in the fields. Burdened ration-carts rumbled by. Guns, each drawn by a team of straining horses, thundered on. Officers in flowing rain-cloaks and mounted orderlies clattered along the stony sidewalks. Infantrymen, grey with mud, tramped with pick and spade. Cyclist orderlies threaded a perilous way, like Cockney youths rushing evening papers through the streets. The darkness in the fields would be rent by a stab of flame and a thud of explosion would follow: it was one of our guns firing at a German position miles away.

Several days were spent in preparing for action. Field-dressings and extra ammunition were issued, and carrying-parties were organized. The battalion had instructions to clear and hold the ground between the River Ancre and the Beaucourt road, advancing on both sides of a railway in a gully. The action was fought on 3rd September.

A sprig of white heather from Sir Douglas Haig was given to Colonel Sceales to bring the battalion luck. Just before the battalion moved off, a messenger came from the brigade with a single copy of a map showing the trenches our men were to assault. We were allowed to keep it for only a few minutes, and then had to pass it on to another battalion. I copied it as fast as I could, a difficult business without coloured pencils and under the spur of time.

It was a very intricate map, and there was a
danger lest ditches and trenches should be mistaken
for the lines to show the slope of a hill. I got my
copy complete, but unchecked, within the time
limit, and passed on the original. I then made
more copies, and these were issued in the nick of
time. I was very anxious when the job had been
done, for if I had left out a trench I might have
sacrificed fifty or a hundred of my comrades. After
our assault had been made, and the battalion had
been withdrawn for a rest, an officer was kind
enough to come and tell me that the map had been
a godsend. I had left out a bit of new trench, but
this was probably not my fault.

The attack, though successful at first, was a very
costly one. The leading companies, going out
from Giant's Causeway, came under heavy
machine-gun fire, and I think it was never quite
clear how far the men went forward.

The enemy's dug-outs were strong, and he had
his machine-guns well arranged. It became very
much of a soldiers' battle, men on both sides firing
at each other at twenty yards' range. There was
also a day-long duel of German heavy trench-
mortars, rifle-grenades, and machine-guns versus
Vickers and Lewis guns. Both the Black Watch
flanks were left in the air, and the survivors had to
come back to the old British line. The only way
to get out wounded was through the railway gully,
and there was heavy fire on almost every point of it.

Dear old Major Rogers had his dressing-station
there, and in fourteen hours of unbroken work,
under continuous shell-fire, he dressed over 400

wounded men. A Catholic padre, Father North-
cote, helped the wounded and comforted the dying,
until a shell-splinter knocked out an eye. This
priest was loved by us all, and as much by the most
hopeless atheist as by the most fervent Catholic.
He returned to the brigade as soon as he could leave
hospital.

The battalion came out at night utterly
exhausted, and went to Mailly Wood to rest in
ancient and badly-holed tents among trees. At
night, with an almost full moon throwing the jet
tracery of tree shadows on the green-daubed bell-
tents and brown canvas huts, the scene suggested
the Wild West. It was cold enough to prevent any
but fitful snatches of sleep, and it was dreadful to
hear men crying out in nightmare. I slept with
the pipers, and we used as blankets large brown-
paper wrappings from orderly-room stationery
parcels.

A little later I had the luck to find an apparently
unoccupied house, and, getting in by way of a
window, my colleagues and I made ourselves at
home. There was a nice snowy-sheeted bed in
one room. At nine o'clock at night, as we were
having supper in front of a blazing wood-fire, in
stumbled a battered, blinking-eyed man, who
might have been a hundred. His fixed stare of
bafflement was pitiful. He began poking about
to see what we had brought into the room. Then
most angrily he denounced us as men who had
broken in. We explained, but he was stone deaf.
I wrote a few words in block capitals for him to
read, and, apparently satisfied, he took a cigarette

and sat by the fire. After a while he showed us a
picture of his son in infantry uniform. Nobody
else came to see what we were doing, and we had
a wonderful sleep.

When the battalion returned to the line it had a
long and trying spell. There were few dug-outs,
just shell-holes linked up, open to a fire that never
died down. I saw many cases of shell-shock, poor
fellows who trembled all the time, and could not
stop it, and were very terrified. But once we had
got to trench-headquarters, after a journey over the
open, with shells going on all the time, we found
ourselves in the deepest trench we had ever seen,
one made by the French. A gallery lay under the
trench level, sheltering the headquarters mess, signallers, and orderlies, orderly-room, and battalion
sergeant-major. It was stoutly shored up with
sawn lengths of tree-trunks. The shell-crashes
above sounded faintly down there.

Casualties were heavy. Two successive shells
hit the same fire-bay, killing eight men. When the
battalion came out of the line it was heart-rending
to see them. They were thin-faced, hollow-eyed.
They could not march, but just shambled along.
Rain now fell heavily, and we slopped about in
pools of mud. Though, of course, I had not the
misery and danger of the men in the shell-holes, I
now had trench-fever and neuralgia behind the
eyes, and much diarrhœa of blood.

There are few entries in my diary during the
battle of the Somme, a sure sign that I was hard-
driven. I have never worked in my life as I did in
those days. It was the dreariest time I ever had.

for, enviable though our jobs were considered, there was little rest or recreation for the orderly-room men, except the rest and recreation of marching from billet to billet or to and from battalion trench-headquarters. I saw few civilians, and went for weeks without hearing a woman's voice. When I came at last on a group of British nurses, their high-pitched voices sounded to me like the screeching of monkeys.

CHAPTER XXIV

THE SCHWABEN

ON October 14th the battalion prepared to attack the north face of the Schwaben Redoubt, a stronghold on a ridge looking down on the Ancre valley, where now flooded reaches glimmered, trees rose from the waters, and wild geese cried incessantly. This crest was the Thiepval Spur, which we had been hoping to capture ever since July 1st. At this time the 18th Division had captured the south face of the Schwaben. Our attack was timed for 2.46 p.m. The men went forward eagerly, too eagerly, and some of the heavy casualties at once suffered were caused by our own curtain of artillery fire. To the right Germans showed themselves above the parapet, and poured rifle-fire among our men until a machine-gun, taken into No Man's Land, began to play upon them. The companies became mixed up in the German trenches, but killed many of the enemy and made many prisoners.

Sergeant Hutton, a man of extraordinary coolness, whose repeated acts of courage and military skill, if they had had the luck to be more picturesque, would beyond any question have won him the V.C. and several bars, showed himself once more a natural leader and a man of indomitable endurance. In spite of very severe casualties it was a triumphant advance.

Great work was done by stretcher-bearers and runners. One runner, Patsy Chevers, was partly Irish, and a great talker. It is on record that one rainy night he put his head inside a wet dug-out, where the colonel was sitting, and with a sudden burst of confidence, probably after a rum ration, said to him: " Ye ken, sir, I'm sorry fur ye. I aye think ye must hae' been accustomed to somethin' better at hame." Such is the printed record of that quaint incident, and perhaps the authority for it was Colonel Sceales, but what Chevers himself told me afterwards was that the colonel said to him: " Chevers, this is very different from the life we were used to," and Patsy replied: " That it is, sir, but it's more different for the likes of you than it is for the likes of us." Poor Patsy came from a very poor home, and that was the kind of thing he would say quite sincerely. He made a most trustworthy runner, and though he was rather a wild-looking and excitable man, one you might expect some day to get shell-shock, he took it very coolly when he was badly wounded about the legs and put in a trench to die. He had a last cigarette, said he would play the game to the end, and he died without one murmur or sign of fear.

The battalion was almost continuously in action for six weeks, in which time it lost about forty officers and over a thousand men. Nor had it yet finished with the murderous Somme. The conditions were damnable. There was, in many

parts, no trench line for either British or Germans
—only shell-holes pitted throughout a wild waste
of mud. There were no communication trenches,
and the trackless approaches to the front line were
constantly shelled. At night the most experienced
runners lost their way. There was a great shortage
of water. Men were so done that, as one of them
said, they could not have stopped two babies in a
pram, let alone a German onrush. But an onrush
over the engulfing mud was impossible. Men lay
in these holes, cursed and prayed, and longed for
water and to get back to safety. But when they
came out they did not curse. They were like men
who had been under some frightful operation, and
were now too weak to do anything but long for
sleep.

On their way out of the line on October 25th
several of our men lost their boots in the mud, the
pull of which was enormous. They had to march
to Senlis, six or seven miles away, in stockinged
feet. I was told of a man who sank to his arm-
pits in the mud, and was trampled to death in the
dark. Lieutenant Currey, who was acting-adju-
tant in Lieutenant Scratton's absence through sick-
ness, went out to lead a water-party to the front
line, but lost nearly every man in the dark.

Looking back on those days and on the physical
torture inflicted upon my comrades, I am amazed
that they stood it all with such heroism. Yet there
were no incidents of cowardice on the part of the
Black Watch. We were still a great battalion.
Colonel Sceales, stern though he was, and had to
be, inspired the utmost confidence. Men like

Captain Stevenson, Lieutenant Scratton, and Lieutenant Currey, always cheerful and efficient, were as much loved as any heroes of old.

.   .   .   .   .

The battalion's last assault on the Somme was on November 13th, when our men captured the great tunnels at St. Pierre Divion, together with many prisoners, and suffered what for the Somme were light casualties, a total of four officers and 148 other ranks. That was a great day for the British. It was encouraging to see a prisoner's cage of barbed wire fill quickly with a thousand prisoners. The privates stolidly attacked their emergency rations. Their clasp-knives had been taken from them, and I helped to open their tins for them and fill their water-bottles. The A.P.M. (the British officer in charge) came up to me angrily and said: " What do you think you're doing?" I said : " I'm letting them eat their own emergency rations, because if I don't our men will give them our rations, and we haven't any to spare."

" Do you think they would treat you like that?" said the A.P.M., and turned on his heel.

In a little while a portly French dame walked into the cage, her apron full of bully beef. The A.P.M. was almost speechless. " What the hell next?" he asked, and had her cleared out. This lady was well known to the soldiers as a kindly old soul who fed the lads on their return from the trenches, and sent them away with good things.

The Germans looked yellow at the first glance. Some must have shaved that morning, and wore clean uniforms. Others told me they had had twenty-one days in the line, and were about done. Many were not more than seventeen, and were on the edge of a breakdown. A party of officers came along just before I left. One, a colonel, was a pleasant, squat, middle-aged man. He was very shaky. There was a keen-eyed little Jew officer, with dark hair brushed hard back, and a habit of wrinkling his forehead in astonishment. Another officer, about twenty years old, in a big German steel helmet, looked like a Salvation Army lassie in a poke bonnet. He was very white, and wore big round spectacles, as did half the captured officers. All the Germans bore themselves with military dignity, and some of them flung coins to the British crowd a little contemptuously. A private who spoke English was asked for souvenirs. He replied that the Black Watch had them all. He smiled when an Englishman said we were going to take Bapaume that night. He told the joke to his friends, and they laughed heartily.

It was a queer sight: that great square outlined in barbed wire on the green hill, a square that was soon blue-grey with Germans. Those officers impressed me. They were not the Prussian type of bully at all, but men of highly-trained intelligence.

.   .   .   .   .

The battle was now being choked with mud. We could not hope to break through till next spring. A frightful gloom began to settle upon us all. I do not think the men could have carried on much longer if they had not hoped that the end was near. The imagination seemed to be unable to look further forward than three months. It *must* be over then.

I wrote in my diary:

PEACE OPINIONS AT THE FRONT.

Front Line: " Peace at any price, for Christ's sake!"

Battalion Headquarters: " Peace soon? Too good to be true. If only——'

Brigade Headquarters: " Ah well, we've had enough of this."

Division Headquarters: " Peace? Oh, not yet. We must have another smash at 'em first."

Corps Headquarters: " No peace, now or ever. Fight on like hell, damn you."

The Base: " Peace likely? I 'ope to Gawd it ain't true. This is good enough for me. It'll suit me for life."

CHAPTER XXV

ON TO YPRES

BITTER as we were at times, and shaken by
constant casualties, it was astounding how
we recovered when we had had a few days'
rest. We moved north to Wormhoudt in French
Flanders. Good old Flanders! Two years before
we were sick of it—sick of the mud, the rain, the
flatness of landscape and trench life. Since then
the battalion had struggled blindly in the Somme.
That maddening battle had worn down the men's
nerves to the quick, and now—how good it was
to be in Flanders again! When, in the pink of
condition, we had marched in midsummer heat
from Le Touret to the battle of the Somme, a
number of men fell out on the way. When we
began the march back north in bad weather and
after exhausting days, not a man complained of
bad feet, not a man thought of bad feet. It was
snowing in intervals of a watery, sunny day, but
the whole battalion was cheerful.

Now we were billeted in and around Wormhoudt, a trim little town of warm-hearted fat
women who talked to us in home-like intonations
of Flemish, and fine little urchins who chattered
in French and English.

After the shell-torn downs of the Somme, where
not a blade of grass lived, and woods had been

blasted to black stumps, this land of windmills and small farms was to us a golden paradise.

Leave came round again. I went to the old family doctor, got something good for my boils, and being hardly able to walk, spent most of the leave resting. I returned to find we were going, sooner or later, to the Ypres salient. Well, anything would be better than the bloody Somme. The battalion moved into trenches at Irish Farm. On New Year's Night the Germans raided the front line, expecting the Scots (so our theory ran) to have got drunk on their annual festival, but our defence arrangements worked perfectly, and the enemy raiders' line of retreat was cut off by heavy British artillery fire. They suffered heavily.

It was not till January 17th, 1917, that we first saw the dead city of Ypres. Though, of course, we had read many columns about it, we were amazed when we got there, not only at the completeness of the shell havoc, but still more at the almost indefensible position of the town, in a wide horseshoe of the enemy's line. German flares seemed to ring us in. I suppose, as for destruction, there had never been so grim and complete a ruin in the history of Europe. We had seen hamlets and villages lying a dishevelment of grey dust and refuse, but here was a town blasted to a broken and blackened skeleton. Cellars and buildings which gave any shelter were used as billets, and many an ugly 60-pounder snout peered out of the window of a ruined house. Outside a dressing-station a dozen cars waited for wounded, of whom there was a never-failing stream. Ypres, plainly, was an unstaunched wound that was likely to bleed till the day of peace. We wondered why it was thought worth while to hold this stinking ruin at such a cost.

We now had the experience, novel to most of us, of being immured in a prison, quite a big one even for a big town like pre-War Ypres. The damp that discoloured the plaster of the walls and the icy winds through an iron-barred window made our stay appropriately penal.

. . . . .

We were very much afraid of gas here. One day about five in the afternoon, a corporal, breathless with excitement, burst into our cell with the cry: " Gas coming! Put on your helmets," and was gone.

We now had the small box-respirator, but not having been trained in putting it on we tugged with fumbling, foolish hands at clips and tubes. To my surprise Neil McDonald had his mask whipped on in a second or two. Norman Robertson struggled grimly. He was in difficulties. I soon got the mask on my face and groped for the mouthpiece. By the time I was gas-proof, an officer had come demanding who the devil had spread the panic. If it had not been a false alarm, most of us would soon have been under wooden crosses. In my struggle to adjust the mask, the clearest thought in my mind was: " Well, we shall die with a foolish smile on our lips, pathetically helpless, and so far it isn't such a bad death after all—if this is death."

Almost at once we were ordered into the cellars, for shells were falling close, and a corporal on guard had been killed and three others wounded. It was a tight crush in the cellars, and under the electric-light we could study each other's expression—usually the expression of children pleased with a novel experience.

Gas, but not enemy gas, nearly had me after all. One morning Robertson and I woke with throbbing heads and vomited repeatedly. We found we had been slightly gassed by the fumes of a charcoal fire in the room next door.

I had to make many journeys along the famous Poperinghe-Ypres road, that road that was like the handle of a spoon, with the bowl representing Ypres in its hollow. German shells killed men of ours every night on that road.

One day I had been up to the battalion headquarters at the salient, where bullets were hissing into the ground of the old familiar way. I had got a little beyond the Asylum, when German artillery opened on the road. The shells were dead on the mark, and the few motor-wagons about put on top speed to get away. It was hopeless to ask for a lift, and certain death to remain where I was. So I made an effort to board a speeding motor-wagon. The back board was very high, but I got a grip of it, and hung frantically, squirming to lift myself up. For three hundred yards or so, whilst shells were whizzing and bursting on the road, I hung on. Then at a jolt over a shell-hole I lost grip with the left hand, and dropped. I ran.

I had no rifle or equipment, only my small box respirator and first-aid haversack full of papers over my great-coat. A shell burst only five yards in front of me, and as I saw the pattern of red fire on the hard ground I felt sure I should be struck, but the greater part of the shell scattered forward instead of backward. Panting along I felt a tremendous excitement and surprise at my own speed. Shells came whining with a loudening cry, to burst viciously with a rain of fragments. After a quarter of a mile or so, when my heart was jumping as if it would burst my breast, I came to two carts drawn up beside an excited infantryman with a flag and "Traffic Control" arm-band.

" My God!" he was saying to the driver, " is that ammunition? You ought to be miles away. Wait till the next shell bursts, then away like hell."

As the wagon dashed off I scrambled on behind, and lay on my stomach on boxes of shells. The horses went furiously, lashed and cursed without mercy. The wagon jumped and crashed and lifted on the shell-pitted road like a ship at sea. Our back-board was riven off by the jolting of the shells, and away went a great box of ammunition on the roadway. I found my legs were insecurely holding a fat shell that was slipping towards the end of the wagon. I was afraid I should have to let it go, for I did not know enough about shells to say whether there was a safety-catch on, and, anyway, the fall of the shell on the road might release it. I had to let it go at last, shut my eyes, and waited. It did not explode.

A moment or two later I, too, was shaken off, and resumed running. Then I got on to a racing G.S. wagon, slipped off at a side road, and hobbled into Poperinghe, my feet sore and swollen with running.

CHAPTER XXVI

WE MUST GO ON

FROM time to time I had a few moments' chat with my old friend John Lee, who now was about to go home for his commission.

Willie Addison, now a lieutenant in an entrenching battalion, came to see us, and had supper with us. After his gallant work on September 25th, 1915, he applied for a commission, and had almost a year and a half of quiet life at home. I was sorely tempted to apply again for a commission, but still felt reluctant to leave the battalion in which so many of my dearest friends had perished. It seemed to me that if I went home for a year and a half this would see me through the War, but I did not want to leave my cushy job and my chums. I wished I had the pluck to volunteer to return to the firing-line, but I could not nerve myself to that heroic pitch. I might have done it in 1915, but not now.

This is what I wrote in my diary early in 1917:

" I suppose men now going about in short frocks will thrill thirty years hence as they read of our adventures—of charging over the dead-littered No Man's Land against the battered German lines, or running hell for leather through a barrage of shells, or bringing in wounded under fire. These readers will envy us our romances of danger. They will hardly realize how dull and dirty war really is, what a fight we have against lousiness and trench inertia, how thoroughly 'fed-up with the whole issue' every soldier is, save, perhaps, a few young gentlemen who, previously aimless, now find responsibility, the exercise of command, and caste exclusiveness, much to their liking . . . For myself I dislike this life, not so much because it is dull and unprofitable, but because it is making the future so dull and unprofitable. The censor has pretty well stifled the journalistic me—it is the people at home who are writing most of the War stuff. But we must go on and not lose heart. We had to fight this War, and we must win it. We must not be disloyal to our dead."

On February 26th, 1917, Joe Lee went home for a cadet course, and I was the one survivor still serving in France of the band of journalists who came out with the 1st/4th Black Watch. Three had been killed, five had got home wounded (one returned and was killed), the others had gone home for commissions.

It was a great wrench when Joe Lee went. He afterwards returned to France, served in another battalion with distinction, and was captured by the Germans, a superior officer ordering surrender to prevent mere massacre.

We were getting many conscripts from home, and I was intensely sorry for them. Many were middle-aged, with wives and families, and to be put straight into action, as many of them were, was beyond all question a far greater trial than we veterans had to begin with. Yet for the most part they made a good show. One day I went up to the line to see an oldish man who had just come out to us and cheer him up if possible. To my amazement I found him quite happy in a shell-hole, drying his stockings on the feet of a German who had been blown up and landed head first in the mud, and whose legs alone were now to be seen.

When we were out of the line life went on in many ways as if no tragedy darkened our spirits. Every night Private Alec Robb solemnly filled the hot-water bottles for the offices at the stores, and the N.C.O.'s would sit down to feast on porridge or tapioca and cocoa. We used to read the papers from home with many an outcry of scorn. There was a good deal of peevish clamour of the destructive methods of the Germans in retreat. A queer sentiment seemed to prevail in Fleet Street that broken church windows were more horrible than broken men's bodies. We read with much amusement of the German factory for turning the dead into lubricating oil, glycerine for explosives, and food for pigs. We did not believe it.

The trenches were now waterlogged, and gumboots were tried. These kept out the wet, but caused many cases of trench feet. It was impossible to light fires near the front line, and therefore food was cooked some distance back, and taken up in containers.

Although our spells in the trenches were normal, casualties were far more numerous than in those golden days of 1915. Still we were in no big battle, and in the rich sunshine our hopes brightened.

CHAPTER XXVII

A MAJOR REPORTED MAD

ONE of our worst times was in the Observatory Ridge sector, because we were dominated by the enemy on Hill 60. The Hooge area was nearly as bad. A comic incident occurred here at battalion headquarters. Major Murray, a good-hearted old bulldog of a warrior, sat down in a heavy bombardment and began to draw lions and tigers in a note-book. The adjutant came in for a moment, looked over his shoulder, and became very white, and went away. Then the Medical Officer and Signalling Officer hastened in, and asked the major what he was doing. He explained that his little son had sent him a note-book with instructions that he was to draw an animal on each page, and he was now doing this to occupy his mind. " Thank God, sir!" said the Signalling Officer. " Scratton said you'd gone mad, and were drawing all kinds of wild animals in your note-book."

Major Murray, although he could look as fierce as a hanging judge, had a heart full of pity. When he was acting as commanding officer, Colonel Sceales being on leave or in temporary command of the 118th Brigade, a very dirty lad was brought before him on some charge of neglecting duty. Lice were crawling about his neck, and he scratched himself continually. He said he did not care a damn if he were shot for cowardice, for he was completely fed-up and miserable. There was probably this to be said for him, that some men seemed to attract vermin more than others: perhaps the "Scots Greys" found their blood particularly juicy.

Major Murray talked to the lad like a father, and soon had him crying. Then he ordered him to be taken to the baths and given a complete outfit of new clothes and a set of fumigated blankets, and told him the charge would be dismissed to allow him to make an entirely new start. I loved the old bulldog major for that fatherly action.

In spite of the formality and severity of discipline, we had in our battalion a true spirit of comradeship among all ranks. Some men, and even some officers, occasionally had more drink than was good for them. One officer was found drunk in a dug-out. There was some plundering from civilians, who were regarded as making scandalously too much profit out of us. Every one of us in the battalion, and even some padres, swore heartily, but the men's failings were few and trivial in the light of their faithfulness to duty. This was largely due to the example of our commanding officer, who was strictly fair to us all, and gave the men all the recreation he could. I am astonished when I hear of charges that in some battalions it was possible to get earlier leave by bribing the N.C.O.'s. Our principle was that the man next for leave was the man who had been longest from home, and there was no deviation from it. I have been even more astonished to read suggestions of widespread immorality among the troops. Occasionally it was possible for our men to go to a house of the Red Lamp, and a few would go, but they did not repeat the visit. They regretted the waste of money on a wholly unattractive experience.

CHAPTER XXVIII

THE ANCIENT INHABITANT

SOMETIMES, when I tramped with speckless boots along the duck-boards of a neatly ruled trench, 1917 pattern, the mood of the Ancient Inhabitant came upon me. Like the village crony who has seen the streets grow out into the leafy countryside, and remembers the tumbledown cottages standing where now a merchant has his mansion, I thought with a certain satisfaction, mingled with a little regret, of changed days.

Two and a half years before, when I did my first turn of sentry in the front line, we thought of trench life as the stagnation of warfare. Then we saw it change in form and spirit, most notably in the development of the continuous offensive—the raids, the multiplication of trench-mortars and rifle-grenades, and the exchange of fire at all hours. Very different was that watchful waiting of 1914-15 days, when you might eat and drink and sleep the round of the clock and hear not a dozen shots.

The chief trench occupation in the first War winter was, normally, nothing deadlier than tea-making. We made tea for breakfast, tea for dinner, tea at tea-time, tea for supper. There was no tinned milk, and rarely sugar, but plum-and-apple jam was abundant, and was mixed with the boiling water. Biscuits and bully were rarely short.

Such a luxury as stew in the front line was never thought of. But now hot meals were cooked in well-protected kitchens behind the line, and taken up in containers. They were much more varied, too. About the time we went to the front, "the best-fed army in history" was an ironical phrase of great popularity among the troops. Few of us could dispute its sober accuracy now.

If our feeding was makeshift then, in comparison with 1917, much more so was the shelter the trenches afforded. The trench was usually shallow and always muddy. If it was raining (it generally was) you rigged up your waterproof sheet with bayonets across a corner of the trench-bay, and sat under it on the firing-step to snatch what sleep you could.

The dug-out at first was a hole cut in the parapet, or the parados, with a sheet or a door across the top. Gradually men became more ambitious and carved dug-outs big enough to shelter the whole body. There were two conflicting schools of opinion on the subject. One had it that a man must always be on the alert in the front line, and not allowed to run the risk of falling into a deep sleep, as the Indians were prone to do when they curled up in holes. The other school held that dug-outs had a great future, worthy of the best engineering skill. None foresaw the succession of fruitful improvements destined to make the dug-out the underground fortress it became.

·   ·   ·   ·   ·

Soldiering was a simple affair of endurance when

the battalion went out to France. After a few
weeks in the trenches, and our experiences in the
battle of Neuve Chapelle, we considered—we
gallant fellows of the Territorial first line—that we
were by no means novices in the art of war, by no
manner of means. None of us had thrown a
bomb, gas was a horror veiled in the future, and
about the only specialists we had, in the Army
sense, were cooks and signallers.

But now it seemed that fighting required a long
apprenticeship. The drafts came up with heads
chock-full of instructions and muscles trained to
their tasks like prize-fighters. Schools of instruc-
tion had become an immense business in the great
world of the army. Every man was a specialist,
in addition to being trained in musketry. This
development had beneficial results both directly and
indirectly. A man who went to school and came
back a certified first-class bomber fought with
increased self-respect.

The greatest change seen in the trenches since
1914, so far as the ordinary infantryman's ordinary
experiences were concerned, was the introduction of
cloud-gas fighting. There was an alertness, a
tenseness, in the trenches we never knew in the old
days.

Gas was a hideous stimulant to our trench gar-
risons. The use of it by the Germans in the agony
of the fight for Ypres, in which we first learned its
diabolical nature, was considered the unforgivable
sin. If the private soldier had been permitted to
choose the form of punishment for the author of
the War, he would have suggested a whiff of gas.

We had now far heavier shelling to stand than in Neuve Chapelle days, but we were well protected against it in deep trenches and strong dugouts, and with that trusted help in facing shrapnel, the tin hat.

In June we had a stomachful of marching in midsummer heat. We left at short notice for the peace and comfort of a training area. We were told it was to be a real rest, no railways to build or dug-outs to make.

The battalion was reorganized on a four company system, and headquarters details marched with A Company. We found ourselves better marchers than the hardy and disciplined warriors. The headquarters company, now split up, always did well on long marches, considering how many old men it contained and how little training it received. There was a certain class-consciousness about the "head lads" that made them too proud to fall out.

We arrived at Esquerdes almost at the same moment as a torrential downpour; most of us undressed after our grilling march and stood rejoicing in this celestial shower-bath.

We had what might be termed a month's holiday, training for what was to be known as the third Battle of Ypres. This training was carried out in the Serques district. When we returned to the fighting area the old tune was being crashed out, our heavies rumbling over to smash wire, Germans searching for a dump close to our camp, the batter of machine-guns keeping enemy aeroplanes off our observation balloons.

There were many casualties when the companies moved into crater fields that smoked with guns and were torn by the constant tumult of shells. An old comrade of mine, D. R. Watt, a merry rascal, who was a pioneer in D Company, had appalling luck. A shrapnel bullet tore out one eye, went through the nose and damaged the other eye. Nineteen men were injured by gas one night, including Wullie Anderson, but he was soon back.

CHAPTER XXIX

A SEA OF STINKING MUD

AFTER quiet months the battalion was again a cheerful sight when it prepared once more to attack. We went part of the way to the line in a great string of motor-buses. We on the top deck grabbed little apples from over-hanging branches, and pelted the occupants of the bus in front.

Our battalion was in the attack that began on 31st July on a very wide front. We were faced with the worst problem we had ever seen. To get to the front line we had to go through smashed fields slobbering with mud and smelling with the corruption of battle that spread for miles and miles. In this sea of stinking mud progress was inconceivably slow. Going to brigade headquarters on 4th August, I found it took me just half an hour to go the last three hundred yards, for the road was at places several feet deep in mud and you had to be careful not to slip into a hidden shell-hole in which you would drown.

How could we hope, under these conditions, to surprise the enemy or concentrate men and guns without severe casualties? Our plans were made with the most anxious care, and it was inspiriting to see how much forethought the commanding officer put into his share of them. Unhappily one of our own side did more harm than any German we ever met. A British N.C.O., who knew the plans for the assault, was taken prisoner, and he gave the enemy many details of the coming attack, including brigade positions, battalion objectives, the place of concealment of British tanks, and the positions of many batteries. I never knew whether he was a German spy, or some shell-shocked wretch from whom the Germans got this information by trickery. No other explanations of an act of appalling treachery seemed possible.

Our men were to push on through Kitchener Wood and St. Julien, cross the Steenbeek river, and dig in on a far bank about two miles from our front line trenches. The men did well at first. Then communication broke down. The tanks stuck. The artillery shelled our own men. German snipers were able to pick off our boys as they dug in. There was a slight retreat, and some of the men, in their struggle through the mud, lost packs, helmets and rifles. Now came an intolerable night of rain and misery.

The brigadier asked for relief. He reported to the division, " We can't possibly beat off a counter. The men are done." The division replied, " You don't have to beat them off. The artillery will smash the counter."

The men were relieved the next night, when soaked through and through and caked with mud. Every bit of clothing was sent up from the quartermaster's stores, together with a double tot of rum for every man.

By this time the battalion was only two hundred

strong, and it went to Hilltop as one company to occupy the old German front line. The British had the worst of luck in every way. Heavy rain was incessant. The battalion again had to advance and remain for three days under heavy artillery fire, and it had to repel repeated counter-attacks. One company was reduced to an officer and six men. Among the dead was that most lovable and glorious of soldier-comrades, Lieutenant Scratton, the adjutant. Others we lost were Patsy Chevers, the lively Irish runner, C.Q.M.S. Hunter, and an old friend of mine in Dundee training days, Sergeant Jock Dewar. The total casualties were 17 officers and 319 other ranks.

Even out of the line, the men had to pig it in unspeakable muck. It was the old Neuve Chapelle conditions: utter weariness, intolerable mud, shaken nerves, and anguished yearning to get away from it all.

My chums and I had a tragic breakfast. The master tailor, Lance-Corporal Moir, was blown to bits whilst standing at a cooker. A little later one or two of us sat down to eat at some boxes in the field. I had to go off early to the brigade, had no time to finish a proper breakfast, but slipped a couple of biscuits into my pocket. I had not gone out of the field before a shell burst at our improvised breakfast table. C.Q.M.S. Forbes had both legs blown off, but remained conscious, and as he was carried away he called out gaily to the quartermaster (Captain McLachlan): " This is another off the ration strength, sir!" He died a little later. Many at home were grieved by his death, for he

P

used to be the rescue man on the beach at St. Andrews, and all the holiday-makers knew him.

I was appointed to Forbes's place as company-quartermaster-sergeant of A Company. I was told I must not feel obliged to take it, since I was considered to be doing valuable work in the orderly-room, but I rejoiced to be able to do a bit more for my comrades. Looking after rations, water, clothes and pay for the men was a job after my own heart.

CHAPTER XXX

MY NEW CHUMS

WHEN I formally reported for my new duties Captain Plimpton gave me a handsome welcome, and insisted on my drinking a peg of whisky for luck. Then I joined the company sergeant-major and sergeants in a tent. The sergeant-major was a quiet little fellow, Thomas Bowman, D.C.M., who had led the attack on the snipers' house at Neuve Chapelle, and carried on month in, month out, with exemplary faithfulness. Then there was Sergeant Dan M'Bride, a stalwart with a broad, honest face, who was about as fine a man as we had in the battalion, both physically and morally. Then there was Sergeant Wullie Smith, whose steady grey eyes and quiet voice won your heart at once. I felt right away that if we survived Dan M'Bride, Wullie Smith and I would be friends for life. Dan came through all right, and to-day is one of the best amateur golfers in Scotland, but poor Wullie was killed in 1918. He was a great lad for enjoying life out of the line, and when he had had a glass of beer he always looked round for a rifle to shoot at something or somebody. One day he was arguing with a man just out from home about the possibility of a bullet penetrating the roof of one of those metal dug-outs we called elephants. Wullie Smith

at once seized a rifle, and shot at the roof. The
bullet came back, and went through the other
man's shoulder. Poor Wullie was very much
grieved about it, but never got over his passion for
arguing about what a rifle could do. He was a
most honest and straightforward man, and the
Catholics among us do not cease to pray for him.

Then there was Johnny Keith, or, as he was
called, in memory of our Indian division days,
Johnny Teek. He knew by heart the regimental
number of every man of his platoon, and called his
roll not by names but by numbers. He had not a
great physique, but he had a great heart, did his
job well, and was with the battalion to the end.
Our great wags were Paddy Reddy, who was
always talkative, and his great chum, Sergeant
Dolan. Then there were good-natured Archie
Anderson, quiet little Lawson, irrepressible Jock
Houston and Watty Anderson, both wonderful
foragers for food, and cheerful Jimmy Jewell. Most
of them had, and all of them should have had,
decorations, but they never had much to say about
how they won them or about their doings in battle.
There was a sergeant in another company, who,
when out of the line, would frequent the canteen
and late in the evening would ask the boys to strike
a light and have a look at his ribbons, of which he
had indeed a magnificent and deserved show. Our
A Company sergeants used to love to jump
on him and tear them from his chest, but the
victim had always new ribbons up the following
morning.

The privates of A Company were a very mixed

lot. Some of them were fathers of families, and
others young devils always ready for fun. Two of
our men were exceedingly proud of their ability to
discover food. One day they carried off a barrel
of beer from an estaminet, and I believe Captain
Plimpton paid the outraged owner for it to save
trouble. The rascals ought to have been grateful,
but the next exploit was to steal chickens belonging
to the officers, and sell them back to the officers.
Captain Plimpton always forgave them, good
fighters that they were. He was a tall, handsome
Englishman, who I think would be one of the
Plimptons of Beverley, an old sporting family of
whom I had heard in my boyhood at Hull. He
never knew that I was a Yorkshireman, too. It
seems strange now that I never mentioned that I
came from the same part of the country as he did,
but we never had a chance for such small-talk as
that. What did it matter whence we came, what
we had been, or who our parents were? To do
our duty and be cheerful about it were the things
that mattered now.

Our discipline was good, but not that of a
Regular battalion. Thus Sergeant M'Bride and
Private Jock Reid, despite the difference of rank,
were as close friends as two sergeants.

I found the work of a company quartermaster-
sergeant mostly attractive. In the nature of our
duties we "quarties" could do much to make a battalion contented. We were responsible under the
company officers for clothing, feeding, and distributing mail to the men. If these duties were
performed slackly or grudgingly, no instructors in

the world could make the battalion the fighting
force it should be.

Feeding the men was not the simple thing it
sounds. The quartie received his company rations
in bulk, some miles behind the lines, divided them
up for the various platoons and detachments, and
then took them up in ration-wagons towards the
trenches, generally under cover of night. At a pre-
arranged point near the line the wagons were met
by a carrying-party and taken on aching shoulders
through usually miry and bullet-singing ways to
the dug-outs.

When Jerry put a shell-barrage on the roads, we
had anxious and perilous hours. We sometimes
left the quartermaster's stores and transport lines
at 4 o'clock in the afternoon, and did not get back
till 8 in the morning—an experience that involved
many miles of tramping, was repeated daily for
perhaps more than a week, and was only part of
the day's work. Back at his regimental base, the
quartie, after scanty rest, turned to his clerical
work. In conjunction with the orderly-room, we
did our utmost to keep up-to-date records, and the
result was a quick disentangling of pay and allot-
ment problems and a satisfied spirit among the men.

We took our rations past many scenes of bloody
memories. In Battle Wood, on the Messines ridge,
it seemed to me the desolation of shell-pocked wilds
was worse than the Somme. The smell of many
dead horses by the rough cart-tracks made even
veterans like my fellow C.Q.M.S., little Finlayson,
vomit. We were much troubled by airmen, for
the blue skies were aswarm with white-gleaming

Germans, who dropped their bombs or fired machine-guns wherever they could harass the troops.

The famous Hill 60, now a mound of smashed dug-outs in the usual battle-field desolation of shell-pits and mine-craters, was too much for the strongest stomach. The smell of rotten flesh was unspeakable. Let us thank God that we do not remember smells as we do words and scenes. Close to my company a shell had flung a German out of his grave head-first into a shell-pit pool, and his legs were still stuck into the air, with a Stafford-shire lying near in halves.

One of our men, on the very day that he received word of a decoration, got hold of a jar of rum to celebrate it, and before morning was found dead. Most of the men said, " What a lovely death!" It was better than that of some of our men, who were terribly wounded far from shelter and succour, and begged to be put out of their misery. There was an officer who had to be held down by his men lest he should kill himself. I am happy to add that he was got out of the battle zone and made an excellent recovery.

CHAPTER XXXI

LIFE IN THE OLD DOG YET

THE line in front of Battle Wood was at this time bafflingly vague. It had been much battered, it had no barbed wire in front, and neither the British nor Germans had much idea of where their opponents were. It was easy to get lost in No Man's Land. Two Germans, humping mail bags on their backs, jumped into a trench held by our friends, the Cambridgeshire Battalion, and were extremely surprised to find themselves prisoners.

Getting up rations to the men was a sort of lucky-bag experience. You might get past the danger points without trouble and return in excellent time without a casualty, or you might have an exhausting struggle. For the most part I was lucky. I came to be known as a lucky man. But I think my wariness had something to do with it.

I had now had two and a half years on the Western Front, and had gained a very fair idea of how the German artillery mind worked. I could tell from the map—or I thought I could, which was just as cheering—on what points Jerry would fire. Thus, if you had a cross-roads on a ridge with a high contour line, you might be certain that he had guns trained on it. All high ground, however peaceful it looked, if it was open towards Jerry's

line, was dangerous. We old hands knew from the
noise they made his different kinds of shells, and
reckoned how many he would fire in one series.
Armed with this knowledge, such as it was,
whether accurate or not, I had no hesitation in
halting my party before crossing a danger-point and
in rushing them over it as soon as I thought I could
count on a lull in the fire. Some officers thought
this a panic plan. They were like an officer who,
to show his contempt for danger, walked one night
on our front line parapet. As he was shot in about
two minutes the lesson he taught us was not the
lesson he meant.

One of my unforgetable days was 24th September, when the battalion had moved into old German
dug-outs and shell-holes in and near Hill 60. We
took up rations in the afternoon, when the shelling
over a wide area was uncommonly heavy, and we
saw many casualties. The point where we had to
dump the rations was on a short road, perhaps two
hundred yards long, on a ridge. There was a battery dug-out where we turned a right angle to get
into the road, and all along the way there were
stores of shells in readiness for something big.

It needed only a glance to warn us that the place
would be shelled at any moment. Newly-killed
horses and wrecked wagons had been dragged to
the side of the road, and the fields were the usual
impassable stinking mess. We galloped our G.S.
wagons to the dumping spot. I looked round to
see if there was a first-aid post near—a precaution
that we old soldiers always took. Then I had the
rations flung off the carts as fast as we could, just

opposite a second battery dug-out. The wagons
were turned, and had no sooner started homewards
than a shell landed on the rations we had spread
out by the road side. I was blown over, and
scrambled to get up, but three different men
tumbled over me in the smoke as they dashed into
the near battery dug-out.

I found myself scurrying on hands and knees to
the other side of the road, and lay down behind
some rows of shells. The road was a flashing line
of explosions. An ammunition wagon was smashed
and overturned. Then a roar in the ammunition
by the battery made it seem that scores of shells
would go up.

I had no time to get frightened, for two
wounded men lay screaming in the smoking road.
I ran back and tried to get one of them into the
battery dug-out, but the dug-out was jammed with
refugees, and I pulled the man round the corner
to get some little shelter. Then I went back to the
other soldier, who was still moaning piteously in
the road, and writhing away from a shell-pit, his
legs a bloody mess. I picked him up, and set off
to run right down the road to the other battery. I
was intensely excited, fearing the shell dumps
would go up, but clear-minded, and kept mur-
muring to the man, " It's all right now, old boy,
it's all right."

The Germans continued to lash their shells on
the road, and I expected it to go up like a mine. I
might have turned off into the fields and got into
a shell hole, but my whole mind was set on reaching
that battery dug-out. My poor comrade was still

whimpering and crying like a child. Then a shell
landed on a dead horse at the side of the road, and
I was whipped and blinded for a moment by the
flying fragments of rotten flesh and bone. The
man I was carrying cried no more. He had been
wounded again by that shell-burst. Then suddenly I found an artillery-man at my side helping
me with my burden. As we reached the battery
dug-out the air was full of whizzing fragments,
and a man who ran out to meet us got a fierce clout
with a shell-case that came spinning.

" Good old Jock," said one of the gunners, " we
never thought you was going to do it." They gave
me tea as soon as I got my wind back, and stretcher-
bearers took over the wounded man.

I heard afterwards that one of our men, startled
when that first shell came, ran at top speed for three
miles before he got self-control. He had been
wounded by shell-fire on the Somme, and was no
longer fit to fight. When I turned again to that
wretched road, I found the other wounded man
had been picked up and taken to an aid-post. The
road was stinking with shell-holes, and the rations
were a black medley of ashes. My guide and
carriers were not to be found, and it was with some
difficulty that I made my way to Captain Plimpton,
the company commander. When I got to his dug-
out he asked at once if I was wounded, for my tunic
was dripping with blood. I explained that I had
been lifting a wounded man out of the way, but he
insisted on my having a small peg of whisky.

As the loss of our rations was serious, the men
being about to go into the front line, Captain

Plimpton said we had better go off to battalion
headquarters on Hill 60. The Germans were
plumping their shells all about us. Captain Plimpton, with his long legs, moved much faster than I
could, and I had to say to him, " Excuse me, sir,
I'm a C.Q.M.S., not a runner."

I expected to have to go right back to a re-filling
point and get rations from there, which would have
meant another ten hours job, but by using some
emergency supplies and what we would borrow
from other battalions, it was not necessary to do
this.

Early in the morning the battalion went up to
the front line, and I brought back a nervy party to
the quartermaster's stores. Owing to the traffic
and the shelling it took us five hours to get through.
The old quartermaster was glad to see me back.
He said, " I can see you've had a terrible time. Get
down to it at once (that meant, go to bed), and I'll
send you a double tot of rum and get you a new
tunic and kilt to put on when you get up. You
can sleep all to-morrow. I'll send someone else up
with the rations."

However, I slept soundly, and was able to carry
on as usual. On the 25th the battalion came back
to Beggar's Wood Camp to refit for action. On
the 26th the boys went over the top to regain a lost
ridge near Bulgar Wood. The orders to the
C.Q.M.S.s. were to take rations up to Rifle Dump,
Shrewsbury Forest. Every ridge on the way was
shelled. The rations had to be carried on the
shoulder for a long part of the journey as the track
lay over a crater area impassable by carts. A leg

sticking out of a jack boot, thousands of shell holes
with dead in them, and two little kilties, with their
arms round each other's neck, as though they had
been carrying something on their shoulders with
two other men, warned us of the fate that always
hung over us.

We had orders to dump our rations at a map
reference. We found this to be a strong German-
built dug-out. Normally, we had to await a ration-
party from the battalion and go up with them, but
that day all we had to do was to leave the rations
to be collected later. It was contrary to our military instincts to leave all that food unguarded, but
in this deathly wilderness there was not the slightest
danger of men coming along to steal. Indeed,
though the battle was going on not far away, it
seemed extraordinarily lonely in that crater area.

The 1st/6th Cheshires dumped rations at the
same point, and my carriers having started back,
I went with a C.Q.M.S. of theirs into the dug-out
to have a rest before starting back. He was a Free
Church Minister's son, but had a roving disposition,
and had spent part of his life as an Atlantic steward.
We began to swap yarns. I told him of some
reporting experiences, such as seeing the detective
going from Liverpool to arrest the murderer
Crippen. He told me of the birds of prey and
blackmailers who haunt big liners. In the midst
of this conversation the Germans interrupted by
rapping the top of the dug-out with a big shell.

My Cheshire friend, who was very calm, said
we had better beat it. We waited for the next
hit, and then dashed to a little trench about fifteen

yards away. This was safer, because the Germans, having made the dug-out, knew precisely where it was, and a few more direct hits would smash it in. Moreover, the doorway faced the German way, and there was a chance of their putting a shell through it. I regretted that I had not hurried off back with the others the moment we had dumped our rations, but the Cheshire was not a bit perturbed. " A direct hit would blot us out," he said, " but otherwise we're all right. It takes hundreds of shells to kill a man."

We crouched in that little trench in the very centre of shell-fire for ninety minutes, during which time one missile followed another so fast that it was hopeless to attempt to make a dash for it. Our trench was ringed with shell-pits at the finish, two of the explosions buried us in a great mess of earth, but we were not hit. When the shelling stopped, we ran until we were well away from the danger point, but Jerry was still hitting the track, and it was not till we had got past Jackson's Dump, a place of furious traffic and unloading activity, that we got into a quiet region.

CHAPTER XXXII

THIRTY-SIX HOURS' FIGHTING

NO sooner had I got under a blanket than aeroplane bombs began to fall around our camp. I hated them worse than shelling. The aeroplane always seemed to be just overhead, and we could hear the bomb swishing down. The ear soon learnt to detect whether a bomb was coming near or not, but at that time that monstrous noise in the night always made us think we were about to be hit. A little rest, and then we quarties had to go up to meet the battalion at Bus House, to give the men breakfast after the battle.

The men on the bayonet strength had gone through one of the worst times the battalion had ever had. On the morning of 26th September the battalion, forming the right of the 118th Brigade, attacked the ridge to the left of Tower Hamlets, where the 41st Division, after severe losses, had been driven back.

Our men fought gallantly, and here and there in the course of thirty-six hours' fighting the line was advanced, but it was impossible to keep control of the action owing to the blowing up of telephone wires and the knocking out of the runners.

Many of our casualties were caused by machine-gun fire from German pill-boxes, a strong kind of dug-out which must be regarded as one of the inventive inspirations of the War.

We quarties, waiting on the road at Bus House, had tea, rum and bread waiting for the men, and had to get them away as fast as we could in motor-wagons to Epsom Camp, Westoutre. The poor wretches, though near exhaustion, were still in that extremely talkative stage which follows a dread experience. As an old reporter, I knew the state of mind well, for I had found that if you could only get quickly to the scenes of colliery explosions or railway disasters the survivors would tell you everything you wanted, but if you got there some hours later, a reaction had set in and they were reluctant to say a word; they just wanted to forget.

The worst news the men had, was that our beloved leader, that great-hearted Yorkshireman, Captain Plimpton, had been shot dead by a sniper just before the battalion was due to leave the line.

Every man was eager to tell me of his own adventures. There was one oldish man whom I never hitherto heard say a single conversational word. He was one of those poor fellows who did their duty but had no joy of companionship and took their misfortune with dumb fatalism. I always pitied such men most, for they seemed to have so few resources. So I listened whilst he told me in full detail, and in tones of astonishment and almost incredulity, how two gigantic Germans had made for him, and he had stood his ground, run his bayonet through one of them, and smashed the other in the chin with the butt of his rifle. He told me this again and again, following me about as I got hold of little groups of men and persuaded them to hurry with their food. I had, at length, to be

severely regimental. Of course, I hated to be
rough with these poor fellows who had been
fighting for their lives whilst I was in comparative
comfort, but it was for their own safety that I
cleared them as quickly as I could from the fast-
filling road on which the Germans might open out
with shells at any moment. Some of the soldiers
who have written books have been bitterly resentful
about the severity of sergeants and C.Q.M.S.s, but
we were not the unmitigated bullies some of the
conscripts thought us. We old hands had learnt a
good deal about war, and knew what we were
doing. I sought out the oldish man the next day,
gave him the nick-name of "Giant-killer" to his
intense pleasure, and so atoned for the martinet
spirit he found in me at Bus House.

We had lost heavily, our casualties being eight
officers and 228 other ranks. The proportion of
shell-shock cases was rising. Two of our officers
were cases of this sort. The veterans considered
Third Ypres was worse than the Somme: it is
rather like saying that one torture of hell would be
worse than another, but there were two added tor-
ments now. First there was the plain evidence that
we were attacking where the chance of success was
well-nigh hopeless. The enemy had the better
position in every way, and even miles back we felt
all the time we were under his eyes. Then there
was a growing conviction that the high command
was incompetent. I did not think so myself. I
disliked the Horatio Bottomley sort of journalism
which was always talking of duds in high places.
It was natural that the poor devils in the slime,

Q

driven to the extreme of misery, should begin to
doubt their commander just as they doubted God.
It gave me no pleasure to see newspapers attacking
the War Office. I knew only too well, being an
old journalist, how easy it was to excite people by
publishing terrific denunciations of those in
authority. I knew also how difficult was our task
to make an impression upon the German military
strength. But this was an exceptional view. Our
men were beginning to be much influenced by dis-
paragements of the high command, and this made
it very difficult to keep our battalion up to its old
standard.

There were not many of the veterans left. Even
the best of all soldiers, though not hit, could not
go on fighting year after year. We had a very
good N.C.O., who, after an action, when details
were being collected for official descriptions of the
battle, began to cry, said he could not remember
doing anything, and supposed he would be shot
for cowardice. I have not the slightest doubt that
he behaved with his accustomed coolness and gal-
lantry, but towards the end got some sort of shell-
shock. He plainly would not be of any more use,
and he was found a staff job. Many of our men
had been wounded once and sent back to the line,
and we could not expect them to be as trustworthy
as before. If a man had been wounded by a
machine-gun he would generally be panicky when
there was machine-gun fire. Similarly, a man who
had been wounded by a shell was unsteady in
shelling. We were getting many conscripts, whose
fighting value, inevitably, was less than that of the

old volunteers. For one thing they were often sent straight into the most frightful experiences, whereas we veterans had been trained by a gradual process into self-control under stress. Then again, many of these poor fellows felt that, as conscripts, they were picked out for the worst duties, and victimized by the N.C.O.s. I do not think this happened in my battalion, but a feeling of injustice rankled among them.

CHAPTER XXXIII

TROUBLE WITH CONSCRIPTS

I HAD my share of trouble with unsoldierly new-comers. It was difficult to force them through shell-fire. One day I was on a duck-board track leading over a swampy region which the Germans could see from a church tower. Had I kept my party of ten or twelve together, Jerry would have plumped a shell into us. Therefore I had to spread my men in a long line, with a trustworthy private leading the way and myself at the end.

Every now and then Jerry put a shell on the boards. One of our men threw down his burden, and began to run back. He said it was simply murder to make men go on under those conditions and he could not stand it any more. I told him not to be a fool, and said we of the Black Watch were not such swine as to leave our comrades in the front line without food. That made no impression on him, and I had to bring out a revolver. I gave him half a minute to think it over, and explained that if at the end of that time he was still determined not to go on I must blow his brains out.

Meanwhile, two other new men had come back after dumping their rations. I ordered them to pick up their rations at once and get on under threat of shooting them too. They were of weaker stuff than the first man, and said they had only come back to see what the trouble was. Then one of them said gamely to the trouble-maker, "Come on, you damn fool. If the old quartie's stuck it ever since the 4th came out, you can surely stick it another half-hour." Thereupon, just within the time limit, the foolish man took up his burden and moved on. He became quite a good soldier. I had several times to use threats, but never had to carry them out. I was not a bloody-minded bully, but was determined that the fighters should be fed. All the conscripts were not unwilling, and some showed fine qualities. My considered opinion is that most men are plucky when they have to be.

Our rest at Epsom Camp was broken every night by bombing aeroplanes, which were greatly helped by the harvest moon. The back areas where we rested were no longer the sanctuaries of healing calm they used to be.

On 14th October, after leaving a camp near Potijze, we were moving down a long, duck-board track across a muddy and shell-torn plain when a German high-velocity gun began firing on it. Our hearts were in our mouths, for there was something uncanny about the speed of the shells. One of these, landing twenty yards, from the track exploded among a group of New Zealanders having tea. One of them was cut in half, and we saw his legs, wide open, flung thirty yards into the air.

Even when we had got out of Ypres and gone in buses to a camp near Locre, German bombing aeroplanes still kept us on tenter-hooks. Whilst we were waiting on the road to be guided to our dug-outs and tents an aeroplane came over and dropped seven bombs in as many half-seconds on a neighbouring camp, killing eighteen men and wounding thirty-three.

We cheered up very quickly on getting to a rest area. I made a note on 18th October that the fighting had quietened down, and it looked as though we had established ourselves in our winter lines, whence, in the following year, with the weight of the fast growing American army beginning to tell, we might come near to ending the War.

But the Third Battle of Ypres was not so easily to die away. The Passchendaele attack had failed, leaving our men to hold a line that might well turn first-class battalions into troops of lunatics. Near Gheluvelt and Dumbarton Lakes, the men had to hold shell-hole posts under conditions of exhausting strain, for the enemy's artillery power seemed unimpaired, and he rained shells and gas upon the poor fellows worming in the mud.

CHAPTER XXXIV

TWO HUNDRED GAS CASUALTIES

AFTER one turn in the front line we had two hundred casualties from gas alone. Going into a headquarters dug-out to make a report, I stumbled over a man in the dimness. He murmured weakly, " Sorry, quartie, it's all right." I knelt down, thinking he was dying, and found his face was black. He murmured, " It's all right, quartie, I'm getting better." He had been gassed, but he was one of our veterans, and would not leave the battalion. He was allowed to lie there, and after a day or two he was able to crawl about again. Almost everyone of us had a whiff of gas about this time.

To get rations up to the Tower Hamlets section we took the carts to Mount Sorrel, where shelling rarely ceased, and then carried our stuff on the shoulder, by ghastly battle scenes, on a duck-board track overlooked by the enemy at Comines. No matter how fierce the shelling became, it was impossible to leave the duck-boards, for the crater area was a waste of churned-up mud, in which lay many of our dead, with the inevitable litter of an advance, such as mules with their bellies torn out, abandoned boxes of bombs, broken rifles, headless corpses, legs, and arms.

Coming back on the first night we had to run

the gauntlet of many gas-shells. There were so many casualties that it was thought best to go up in the morning when mist baffled the German observers at Comines, but we were always in danger at Mount Sorrel, and in that evil valley of the dead, Bodmin Copse. This was the most sinister place I ever saw. The ground had been smashed into a swamp in which many wounded were drowned. The track was broken every few yards. In one shell hole were a machine-gun crew who came down head-first into the mud; their legs were still sticking up from the slime.

I heard an extraordinary story of a wounded man's tenacity of life. It was said that, though he had both legs shattered, he rolled in from No Man's Land, passed our front line without being noticed or noticing it himself, and reached a battalion headquarters, a mile from where he was hit.

The tenacity of some of the wounded was, indeed, astounding. A man would struggle towards safety when almost unconscious. Thus my friend, C.Q.M.S. Campbell, when wounded in High Wood, and paralyzed down one side, crawled six hundred yards among the many dead, and having left a wounded chum planted rifles and spades every yard or two in order to guide stretcher-bearers back. He hardly remembered doing it, but was told afterwards that he had planted a straight row of rifles showing the way clearly as a line of white tape, and his chum was brought out.

Late in October came a startling piece of news. Lieutenant-Colonel Sceales was to leave the battalion to take command of a Tank Brigade. He

was such a master of method that I had always
believed he ought to command a much higher formation than a battalion, but he had grown so much
a part of the 4th/5th Black Watch, in spite of his
coming to us from the 1st Argyll and Sutherland
Highlanders, that we expected him to stay with us
to the end and to ride at the head of the battalion
on a triumphal march through Dundee when the
War was over.

He was a gallant and most loyal leader, one
always ready to subdue his personal ambitions to
the interests of the battalion.   He was eager to
acknowledge good work.   On two occasions he had
printed at home special battalion orders in which
he recorded the names of those who had shown
gallant and great devotion to duty, with a small
category of those who had done exceptionally good
work.   At the same time he knew that much good
work must pass unnoticed, and he made us all feel
that it was a high honour to be a soldier of the
Black Watch, as, indeed, it was.

We were more like a Highland chief and his
faithful fighting men than an ordinary battalion.
We had an intense self-respect.   We were not men
going helpless to our doom, but men of honour
who meant to do to the end our sworn duty.   The
worse the conditions the more the battalion steeled
itself to overcome them.   This is not the vain-
glorious claim of a militarist, but the simple truth
as seen by one who was not a militarist, not much
of a soldier, and hated war.   Colonel Sceales was
succeeded by Major T. D. Murray.

CHAPTER XXXV

LIFE-LINES IN THE MUD

NOVEMBER rains came to increase our men's hardships. Even on the Somme our men had not been put to such a prolonged strain as they were now. What little rest we had had since July was amid mud and the unending growl of guns. We had had nothing like the famous holiday at Allouagne. The Kitchener battalions, which we had hoped would come to lighten our load, had done nobly and endured slaughter, but we Territorials were wanted more urgently than ever. We had few hopes of ever getting out of the line for any long rest. Leave was now the one thing we lived for. Better to us than any newspaper reports of victory was the promise made in the House of Commons by Mr. MacPherson that everyone with twelve months' service in France should have leave. I have forgotten all about that politician except that once he was a hero to the British Armies in France.

The Tower Hamlets Ridge, where we did several more tours of duty, became a worse crater swamp than ever. It was still under enemy observation and frequent shell-fire, machine-gun fire, shell-gas attacks. We put down duck-board tracks, but in many places, even if the enemy did not destroy the track with shell-fire it sank into the

mud. The struggling infantry had to carry life-
lines lest they should be sucked to death in the
soft, engulfing mud. It was common for men to
have their gum-boots pulled off by the suction,
and we suffered from the cold and damp.

The enemy's favourite targets in this area were
Mount Sorrel and Jackson's Dump, and we generally ran past these points. The worst trip I had to
the trenches with rations and back took thirty-one
hours. When I got home to the transport lines the
store-men had to cut the mud-clogged boots and
socks off me : the hose-tops had already been drawn
off by the mud in some shell-hole. I then had to
return to the trenches, for rations had to be got up
every day. When the men came out of the line
all their puttees and socks had to be cut off. I
never saw them in a worse plight of exhaustion.
They got a rest of only four days, but next time
were sent to less muddy trenches. We then
employed mules to carry the rations. They were
able to go further than the carts, and so helped to
spare our much-enduring carriers. They were
uncommonly tough beasts, and were not afraid
of shell-fire as horses were.

On returning from Bodmin Copse I had to
run through barbed wire to avoid shells that were
hissing out gas on the track. I got a few scratches,
and these turned to septic sores that put me out of
action for a day or two. I rested on a day of blustering wind, rain, and slobbering mud, while my
faithful storeman, Lance-Corporal John Ballantyne,
a printer from Hawick, took up the rations to the
line. He was a quiet, faithful little fellow, and,

like all our printer soldiers, a credit to his craft.
I was anxious about him, for he might have had
to face mutinous conscript carriers, but he came
back in good time and reported a cushy trip. He
survived for several months after this, and was then
killed.

Here let me pay tribute to another printer who
was a willing and cheerful worker, one Private
Cakebread, whom we called Jane, in memory of
the famous London character who was always getting drunk. He used to make up (in the technical
printing sense) the pages of *Sketchy Bits* or *Photo
Bits*. He was a thin, stooping, white-faced man,
not soldierly to look at, but a non-stop worker.

．　　　．　　　．　　　．　　　．

When the outlook was darkest and we were
bracing ourselves up to face a killing winter, there
came the news of a great British victory by the free
use of tanks at Cambria. We soon learned that the
Germans had smashed their way back, but the
advance into green country open to cavalry was a
great tonic at the time, better than we looked
for.

Very soon we were back in France for a rest.
The battalion came out of the line on 25th November. We travelled part of the way in railway
vans, and arrived at a collection of dirty and
draughty hovels known as Alberta Camp about ten
o'clock at night. The cooks, moving on in
advance, had prepared porridge; tea and rum were
issued also. The men, exhausted but happy,

settled down for the first real sleep since a week before, but were called up at 3 a.m.

The youngsters, suddenly aroused from alcoholic slumber, were nearly all sick, and it was an unhappy crowd that trudged down the starlit road to the railway, whence a short train journey brought us close to Terdeghem. The men shambled with bent heads, all but done. Billets proved to be cheerless draughty barns. Men were allowed to sleep until four in the afternoon, when the cooks arrived with a steaming meal, pork and beans, potatoes and onions. Having got all my records up-to-date, and the company being fast asleep, I took Lance-Corporal Ballantyne into the village, and we got a Frenchwoman to give us a lunch of eggs and chipped potatoes, bread and butter and coffee. Terdeghem was then a village of British Army training schools, and in our dirty tunics and kilts we felt like tramps among spick-and-span gentlemen.

The promised rest proved the usual delusion. Some new clothing was issued, we had a pay-out, and we were a little cleaner and less deadly tired than we were, but when, on November 29th, we were ordered to Brandhoek, near Ypres, presumably for working-parties, we had the inevitable sense of cheated hopes.

We found Brandhoek a place of misery, with torn tents and no floor-boards. There was a hard frost, but we could get no material for fires. It grew so savagely cold that I told one of the storemen that he simply must find some fuel. He and other bright foragers were absent for a while, then came back with sparkling eyes and loads of wood. I could see from their mischievous faces that it was best not to inquire where they had got the stuff. In the morning there was a great hubbub because a general discovered that his private lavatory had vanished in the night. He never learned where its wooden walls had gone.

CHAPTER XXXVI

A ROW ABOUT RATIONS

ABOUT this time there occurred an incident which, trivial though it then seemed, was to be a turning-point in my life. We quarties had made up our rations, and were taking them to the companies. One of the regimental police met us, and ordered us to go direct to the commanding officer while his men took charge of the rations. We had no suspicion that anything was wrong. We four quarties were all worn-out veterans who got on well with the men, being, in the old Army phrase, both mothers and fathers to them. We were kept waiting for a long time at battalion headquarters, and then were summoned into the presence of the commanding officer. It looked like a court-martial. All company commanders and the sergeant of police were there.

Major Murray said he had heard with extreme disgust a complaint that we were giving the officers shorter rations than we gave the men. He could not believe such a grievous charge, but in order to test it he had had all rations that day diverted to battalion headquarters, they had been opened by the police in his presence, and he had found that in some cases we had given the men more than we had given the officers. Taking A Company, he said I had given the officers no butter and no jam, although the men had both. What was my explanation?

The explanation was extremely simple. Officers were entitled to no more rations than the men. Most of the rations were delivered in tins, and as soon as I got them I worked out what each man was entitled to. Thus it was a common thing for a tin of jam to serve six men and a tin of butter to serve twelve. If there were three officers in a mess I did not give them a tin of jam and a tin of butter each day, but a tin of jam every other day and a tin of butter every fourth day. I kept a record of the ration proportions, and could have proved that this was my just method.

When the commanding officer asked whether the company commander accepted my defence or wished to bring further evidence against it, he at once admitted that he had not looked at the matter in that light, and had no doubt that what I said was true.

The other C.Q.M.S.s made similar statements, and the commanding officer said we had cleared ourselves, and could take our rations away.

We often found in the War that what worried us most were not real sufferings, but silly little things, and I am ashamed to say now that we were much more touchy about this incident than we need have been. We had been given a fair trial, and vindicated ourselves, but we were nettled, chiefly because we found the complaints had come from newly-arrived officers who had not joined the Army until long after we had been fighting. It is not my way to let people attack me with impunity,

and I could not help saying to an officer who was
defending his action, that, after being trusted by
men like Colonel Walker and Colonel Sceales,
Major Kennedy, and Mr. Scratton, I objected to
being tried as a thief and swindler on the worthless
evidence of men just out from home. Finally, I
said if I was not to be trusted with rations, I was
willing to revert to the rank of private and be a
fighter again as I had been before some of these
officers knew what fighting was. In fact, I was
rather theatrical, and enjoyed myself. It was not
often that I could let myself go. My company
commander spoke to me tactfully about it, and
apparently the incident, a trifling one in our life-
and-death struggle, was about to end. But there
was what I took to be a sequel. Word came that
the commanding officer was willing, if I wished it,
to recommend me for a commission. It looked as
if I were to be promoted out of the way. Before
I made up my mind I was given leave, from
2nd to 16th December, 1917, the longest spell of
furlough I had had since I joined the Army.
C.Q.M.S. Campbell was one of my companions
on the journey home. We were both a little
panicky whilst waiting for the train to start at
Poperinghe, for the Germans had killed seventeen
men in the train the night before.

My wife and I spent the leave partly in
Edinburgh and partly at Dundee, where we made
a point of going to the homes of men in my company, and passing on messages from the front. I
called on many of those whose sons or husbands
had been killed, and said what comforting words

R

I could. One woman turned on me with cold anger. " Yes," she said when I had finished, " and when all your fine words in your fine English voice are done, how are they going to help me buy bread?" The poor creature was almost distraught by brooding over her loss, and I am afraid, try as I would, my visit of sympathy merely inflamed resentment.

One other incident may be related here to show how difficult it sometimes was for soldiers and civilians to understand each other in those years of stress. A comrade had been killed on the German wire. I wrote to his people giving them a guarded account of his death, and telling them what a good soldier he was. The father wrote back and said it was very suspicious that I had not mentioned the funeral : surely his son had received the tribute of Christian burial, and he would like to know which of his comrades had attended. I explained that the boy had been killed close to the German trenches, and the Germans were sure to take in his body for burial. The father wrote back a letter angrily condemning me for not bringing back his son's remains.

To us at the front, accustomed in a day's journey in the crater area to see the unburied remains of hundreds of men, it seemed amazing that people at home should imagine we could risk the lives of three or four men to bring a body across No Man's Land. There are times when I doubt whether any who were not there will ever realize the conditions on the Somme and in the Salient.

For the most part everybody I met was

extremely glad to see a man from Dundee's own battalion. I never felt that dislike of civilians which some soldiers undoubtedly developed. But I was increasingly awkward in society amid glib civilian talkers who knew just how Haig ought to have punched holes through the German line.

.   .   .   .   .

On return to the battalion I found it resting at Belle-Houllefort. It was exhilarating to tramp the frost-bound roads amid the sheen of sunlit snow-fields and the brown and green tracery of the woods. At night, under a full moon, there was a memorable beauty in the greeny-white wastes and silhouetted trees.

On Christmas Day the company had a rabbit stew for dinner. Being English, I felt that something more must be done to mark the day, and with Corporal Hird, a Fife miner, I trudged ten miles to Boulogne. We had difficulty in getting a meal, as the *estaminets* were not allowed to open until 6 p.m., but we found a woman who was willing to give us steak and chips in a frowsy back parlour. Afraid lest the military police should find us, she would not give us a lamp, but left the tap-room door open to let us see dimly what we were eating. The only drink we could get was stout. Then we were stealthily put out by a side entrance, and went to a picture theatre, where Kipling's "Light that Failed" was screened. We walked back to billets through ten miles of blizzard.

We had an official Christmas dinner on the

26th, when the menu was Scotch broth, beef-steak
pie and roast potatoes, mince-meat pie, plum-pudding, and stewed figs, apples, nuts, oranges, and
beer. Officers and N.C.O.s waited on the privates
in accordance with an old Army custom. There
was plenty of jollity and fun, for once out of the
line men soon tired of talking of horrors, and
joined in sport and friendly drinks. The local beer
did no great harm. Though I did not touch it
myself, I had now abandoned my teetotal prin-
ciples as thoroughly as my vegetarianism. No one
who saw how the rum issue cheered the men, and
all the enjoyment for which it stood in a tedious
day of discomfort, would have wanted to stop it.

CHAPTER XXXVII

I FIGHT A MADMAN

WHILE in this area I had to fight for my
life, unarmed, against a man who charged
me with a bayonet, one of our own corporals.

I can see him now, with round, mournful eyes,
black hair, and a lean, powerful body. He had
had bad news from home. His trouble shook him
more than we thought, and when, on this rest, he
was able to buy rum from the local peasants, his one
aim was to drink himself to forgetfulness; he
became almost a madman. He was especially
embittered by being repeatedly reduced in rank and
being subject to a company sergeant-major who had
only just come out from the reserve battalion at
home. It was a grievance with many good
N.C.O.s that though they had been fighting for
three years, till their nerves were gone, they might
find themselves, as in this case, under the orders of
a man from home who did not know what fighting
was.

The corporal had got it into his head that the
sergeant-major had a malignant animus against
him, but I am sure this was quite untrue. The sergeant-major, like most men, was brave enough
when put to it, and was a good comrade.

We had gone to bed when I woke in alarm, as I

often did, being at this time very nervy. I sat up on the straw of a little stable I shared with the sergeant-major and peeped out through the doorless but roughly waterproofed entrance on the great frozen square of manure that formed the centre of the farm. The corporal, in his shirt and with bare feet, and muttering threats, was rushing with rifle and bayonet at the port across the manure. As I sprang to my feet he charged as fast as he could. I had only just time to step aside and then fling my arms round his waist.

I realized that it was the sergeant-major he was after, and shouted at the top of my voice while I struggled with the panting madman. Just in time a brawny sergeant came to the rescue and threw the corporal on his back.

Though we must have made an alarming uproar, the men packed tightly and sourly in the other outbuildings did not awake. We made the wretched corporal fast. After a time he broke down utterly. He was intensely sorry he had attacked his old quartie, and after a while I was able to make him shake hands with the sergeant-major. We arranged to say no more about it.

In the morning, sobered, he was more morose than ever, with scarcely a word for anyone. When the company went again into action he was killed.

I doubt whether any one else alive can say that he fought, unarmed, against a man with a bayonet and escaped.

New Year's Eve found us breakfasting at 11.30 p.m. in readiness for an early start back to the fighting front.

Our route was Seminghem Canal Bank (of evil memory to my battalion), and Irish Farm, near Ypres. The frozen roads made it a trying journey, though we had the train from Wieserne onwards. We encamped in huts and tents at Irish Farm, only a few yards from what was our front trench on 1st January, 1917, when the Germans raided that part of it which was held by A Company. The scene was now one of extreme transport activity, with trains and wagons well in the foreground.

Whilst there I received what was a very rare message for a N.C.O., a telegram from home, for usually letters arrived quicker than telegrams. My correspondent was Mr. Herman Lee, who reported that my old friend Joe, who, as an officer in another battalion, had been taken prisoner at Cambria on 30th November was unwounded, and well at Karlsruhe.

The battalion had a freezing time in the trenches. A company was in shell-hole posts for two nights, and then in support for two nights.

My company lost an officer and his servant and two N.C.O.'s, but this tour (that is, turn of duty) in the line was considered uneventful.

There was to be one more tour, and then the battalion would end its fourteen months' stay on the Ypres front. Our division, the 39th, had the longest spell of any in the Ypres salient. High official tribute has been paid to the way we got the rations and water up to the men during the whole time in the salient, where the fact that the Germans could see us coming, made the task one of great difficulty and danger at all times.

Just before the battalion was going into the line for almost the last time during this prolonged stay in the Ypres salient, word came that I was to go home for training as an officer. I wrote in my diary: " Joy at the prospect of going to Blighty is tempered with regret at leaving good comrades and congenial work after three years in France and Flanders."

Not only was I the last of the *Advertiser* group that went out with the 1st/4th Black Watch, but I was one of the very few men, possibly the only one, who had been with the battalion all the time. Some men of the original 4th had gone home wounded, or been transferred to other units, and had returned to us, but I had never left the unit for a day except on leave.

It was a wrench to leave the old battalion after being in it for three years and five months, almost three years of it in France and Flanders, during which time the battalion must have had close on three thousand casualties. I had made warm friendships in the 4th and 4th/5th, had many happy hours, and known heroic and lovable men. But it seemed unlikely that I was leaving the regiment for ever. I expected my training to take four months, and I should then return, for I felt sure the commanding officer would second my efforts to get back to my own battalion.

We left Hilltop Camp for Hospital Farm on 15th January, amid a downpour, to find out new quarters deep in mud with an inch of water on the

hut floors.   At ten o'clock at night I was ordered
to England.   I had hardly time to say good-bye
to a single friend, caught the leave train at Elver-
dinghe with a minute to spare, spent the 16th at
Calais, and crossed on the 17th.

CHAPTER XXXVIII

ANXIETIES OF A CADET

IN London I was given a fortnight's leave, with orders to report on 10th February, to the G.O.C., Lowland Reserve Brigade, Bridge of Allan. A day or two later I received word that I would join the 5th Reserve Battalion, Highland Light Infantry, Cornton Camp, Bridge of Allan. I went home to Dundee, and the family doctor was called in to treat my persistent septic sores. Gradually I became more fit than I had been for many months. The Army seemed in no hurry to have me back, and it was not until my leave, extended more than once, had lasted for twenty-five days, that I had to report to the orderly-room of E Company, 5th Reserve H.L.I.

I felt very unhappy on my way there, like a small boy going to school for the first time, but the sight of Black Watch kilts cheered me up, and I found to my delight that Dan M'Bride was reporting there too. I imagined I should be a poor sort of soldier among the V.C.s and D.C.M.s and Old Contemptibles I expected to find, but I need not have been so modest. My record turned out to be quite an unusual one among men who, for the most part, had only been out a few months before being sent home for commissions. Many of them said they had no hope of passing the examinations. They had only applied for commissions in order to get a rest from the Front.

My wife travelled with me, and took rooms close to the camp. In a sense this was our first home together, and, after the strain of the Salient, I found life here as happy as could be. For a change we used to go to the Bridge of Allan Hydro for dinner and a dance, but our best times of all were in our little rooms, playing bridge with Dan M'Bride and another Black Watch man, Corporal George Hutchison.

Parades were over by four o'clock every afternoon. Sometimes the day's work ceased even earlier, for the Allan Water, famous in song, usually a narrow, swirling burn, used to flood our training-field. We never had to march through floods, and we came in if it rained. It was startlingly different from the Front.

We had no heavy training at Bridge of Allan. It was a receiving depôt, and we marked time until we could go on to a cadet school. We did the usual saluting drill and platoon and company drill, and went for route marches in that historic countryside, where the Callander Hills, rising in massive outline against the winter sky, were crowned with the gleam of snow.

A draft of fifty cadets left for Gailes on 8th March, but Dan, Geordie, and I were not in it. We felt now like old boys, or at least like second-term boys, and we were not eager to give up our semi-civilian life.

Then, like a shell-burst, into our dreams came news of the 5th Army disaster. Dan and I knew

that our old battalion was in it, and we could tell
from the officer casualties in the papers that our
own company had suffered heavily. No word
came from the sergeants, though they had promised
to write. It was evident that our beloved old
4th/5th was going through times of agony, and
we not there.

Those were days of the utmost depression for all,
but especially for men like Dan and myself, just
home from a unit now in grave peril. We expected
to be ordered back any day, probably to go back
as company sergeant-majors, possibly even as
officers. We did not imagine the full disaster that
had come, or that we could never have got through
the chaos to the remnants of our old battalion.

Still we remained at Bridge of Allan, and this
strengthened our fears that we should be rushed
back to our units in France, for, obviously, if we
were to have the usual full training of officers,
we ought to be getting on with it at the cadet
school. Then we heard that mumps had broken
out at Gailes, and we had to stay at Bridge of Allan
till the quarantine was raised—a pleasant fate when
spring had begun to light the cottage gardens, and
the fields were starred with daisies and buttercups,
white lilies and daffodils brightened our table, and
snow gleamed on Ben Ledi and the Ochills.

Food was becoming much dearer. We paid 4s.
a pound for salmon, which seemed to us calami-
tous, and chocolate creams cost about a penny
each. I solemnly protested in my diary when I
had to pay what seemed then the scandalous price
of 9d. for a hair-cut.

No word came from the 4th/5th Black Watch, but the newspapers reported that my old commander of the 118th Brigade, Brigadier-General E. H. C. P. Bellingham, was missing, and understood to be a prisoner in Germany.

May came, and we were still living our easy life at Bridge of Allan. Those of us who had rooms in the town frequently broke out of camp by going in the dark down the riverside instead of by the road. A friend would answer for us at roll-call, and make up pillows and packs in the bed to represent a sleeping man when the officer paid his last visit of inspection.

We were often threatened with "R.T.U.", an expression that was to become very familiar to us. It meant "return to unit". That dire punishment, the cadet's extreme penalty, was to be exacted for any breach of discipline whatsoever. We ought to have felt cold fear at those initials, but we didn't. The Major, our hawk-eyed, hawk-beaked company commander, read out solemnly on parade, as though he loved it, a War Office letter instructing commanders of reserve battalions to relegate all unsuitable prospective cadets to their units, whether for medical unfitness, inefficiency in platoon drill after one month's training, or any breach of discipline whatever. " This is the letter, these are the instructions," declared the Major, in his best Sheriff Court manner, learnt in practice at Glasgow, " which will be acted on in future without hesitation." Then he reminded us that what might be a trivial error of conduct in an ordinary soldier was a gross breach of discipline in our exceptional case.

And the world went on the same.   A few jests at "getting the wind up", at the major's death sentence manner, and the stern warning fell dead. Joyous youth refused to be cowed by threats of France from officers who had never been there. In reality we had no grievance against the Major, and for all I know he may have had distinguished service at the Front, though some of our instructors had not. He was quite a likeable man, in spite of his forbidding appearance at orderly-room.   He had a difficult task to keep us in order in our reaction from the strain of France. Our physical jerks instructor said : " We're all home for a good time whilst it lasts."   Another officer said : " Nothing worries me except going over the water."   A sergeant-instructor, recalling the dangers "out by", said the main thing was " to keep your head down, and don't volunteer for a single damned thing."   This line of thought was a shock to Dan M'Bride and myself, and quite out of keeping with the spirit that prevailed in our old battalion. We were indignant that we should be threatened with a return to it as though it were a penal establishment.

CHAPTER XXXIX

FUN AT GAILES

PANSIES came out in our little garden, and close by a cherry tree flowered into foamy white. The excitement of uncertainty about the next move was stilled on 7th May, when two hundred of us were named to leave for Gailes on the 10th. We duly passed the doctor, and made out statements of clothing and necessaries. We went off in high spirits at the prospect of becoming real cadets, entitled to wear clothes made to fit, and the white cap-band of nascent officership. We carried packs, great-coats, suit-cases, and golf clubs. When we got to Gailes Camp, on the windy links of Ayrshire, we were met by predecessors from Bridge of Allan, who encouraged us with stories of the ease with which the examinations could be passed. Some of them were in "glad rags", the tunic and so forth of an officer, with a white band round the bonnet or hat, to show the rank of cadet.

Lunch was served with a degree of comfort unknown in the food scrambles at Cornton. W.A.A.C. waitresses, table-cloths, soup-plates (just think of it, soup-plates), flowers on the table, were something new. In the afternoon we explored our surroundings : a beach of dips and hollows and sand, a clear view of the dark-browed island of Arran due west, and Irvine smoking furiously to

the north. Inland, high ground, on which perched
the square bulk of Dundonald Castle, attracted the
eye.

Whilst we were at dinner a senior company
raided our sleeping huts, and upset every bed, and
all our belongings in almost inextricable chaos.
This was always done to a new company. We
soon smoothed down into the grooves of cadet life
in huts and lecture-halls at Gailes. Regulations
appeared intricate at first, but traditional knowledge imparted by our predecessors, who had the
wisdom of two months' experience, led us through
the mazes. After a full working week we felt
ready in our turn to tutor the raw recruits.

We had very little time to ourselves, and I could
do virtually no reading, not even a daily paper,
much less a book—something of a hardship to a
man who had done his best to keep abreast of books
and papers for at least sixteen years. If I had to
die, well and good, but I did not want to go back
to journalism with great gaps in knowledge that
was essential.

In most respects we found Gailes first-rate.
There appeared little risk of anyone failing to get
his commission, the standard being pretty low.
The officers and instructors were men of fighting
experience who were home for a rest. They had
no motive for pressing us too hard.

It was a different atmosphere from that which
we had known hitherto. Moral self-possession,
esprit de corps, great zest for games, respect for
etiquette, were all looked for—in a word, the
officer spirit. We were told that a private had to

do just what he was told, but an officer was expected to act in a certain spirit without being told. The private must be watched : the officer must be as conscientious out of sight as when the commanding officer was at his elbow. We responded readily to this code, and did not break out of camp.

CHAPTER XL

OUR company commander was Captain L. G. Lawrence, whose lectures to us were amusingly outspoken. One of his points was that when the original British Expeditionary Force went out and established contact with the enemy the airmen reported that the roads leading to Mons were crammed with German troops, transport, and guns, but the Staff said this was impossible, and went on. The result was that the British were almost surrounded. He told us the Germans could have taken Ypres in 1914 had they not attacked at Arras and La Bassée at the same time. When the Germans first used bombs the British sent to the R.E.s, six miles back, for bombs with which to retaliate. When these came up nobody knew how to use them, and the R.E.s themselves had to come up to throw them. He said Neuve Chapelle and Loos were almost disasters of bad Staff work. He thought we should have broken the German line at Loos if the 2nd Division had been supported by seasoned troops instead of raw new-comers. He thought the holding attacks of 1915 were so much futile bloodshed. He considered that, for discomfort, the first winter was the worst of the War: it was biscuit, bully, and plum and apple jam all the time. As a characteristic blunder of the Staff, he mentioned the way we allowed the Germans to build the Hohenzollern Redoubt. He saw the building in progress day after day, and asked for artillery to shell it, but was always told it was to be blown up on the morning of battle. The Germans were allowed to spend so many weeks of precious labour upon it that at the time of that lecture the Redoubt still stood, in spite of heavy shelling upon it.

He thought the Battle of the Somme worked badly through lack of unity of command, but, as the Germans held their front line strongly, they must have lost very heavily in our bombardments. He explained that the object of the Passchaendale battle was to deprive the enemy of Ostend and Zeebrugge. Haig had always wanted to advance on and from Passchaendale, but was hampered by the need of conformity with French plans.

This hardly satisfied those of us who had been there, for what we could not understand was why the action was kept on when it seemed out of the question that it could succeed and the advantages were so much in favour of the Germans. The fact was that, as Captain Lawrence admitted later, the science of war had not yet found a sure way of breaking through the German defences. He declared it was a great blow for Germany when Mr. Asquith was succeeded by Mr. Lloyd George, and it was at once followed by German peace proposals. Captain Lawrence advised us not to place any faith in the papers, which were all drivel, and not to expect peace before the summer of 1919.

The lecture made a deep impression on my

fellow-students, and it became the custom with junior officers never to mention the Press without sneering at it. I held, and still hold, that whatever false impressions the Press gave arose chiefly from the news supplied to it officially, and that, so far from being all drivel, it played a great part in keeping up national courage. Nor did I fail to protest against the military disparagement of Mr. Asquith, of whom I knew more than most people in the battalion, having been news editor of the paper that helped him most in his Fife constituency.

We had a deplorable sermon from a Church of England priest, a young wiseacre, who declared that there was no smoke without fire, and he felt sure that the allegations in the notorious Billing case were well founded, especially with reference to those who had been our so-called leaders. The cadets present took this to mean chiefly Mr. Asquith and believed that he was little better than a traitor. This anti-Asquith prejudice was general in the Army. When Britain's staunch old leader was thus condemned, everyone was ready to applaud, but when I defended him I was told that cadets had no right to talk politics.

The June sun sparkled on the crinkling, blue waters, but no one went down to bathe. Why, I did not know, except that there was a fashion in such things. Day after day I proposed going down for a dip, and day after day men shrugged their shoulders at the idea. Then, with one accord, dozens of us went together, discovered unexpected delight on a smooth beach, and vowed we would never let a day pass without plunging into the cool blue of the Firth. We generally took a Rugby ball with us, drenched each other with violent passes, and rushed back, tingling, to dinner. The bathe was the best thing of the day at Gailes.

We had our first examination in June, and went to it with jumping pulses and shaking hearts. Our tremors were not justified by any difficulties in the papers set. Every man must have obtained at least seventy per cent, and some must have got full marks.

CHAPTER XLI

AFTER this the tension began to slacken and my wife took rooms in a miner's cottage at Shewalton, a mile or so from the camp. All was going well, when Spanish influenza swept down upon us. This was a detestably weakening malady, and I do not think the authorities knew quite how to deal with it. Some men in a neighbouring camp were sent to hospital with it and died. We invalids were put in tents in fields, received little attention, and recovered. I got back just in time for the mid-term examination, and, having missed many lessons, did not pass well.

About twenty failed, and six or seven of these were returned to their units. One of them became a casualty in France within a few days. This was a sobering reminder of the perils we had to run, for in our little self-centred world of Gailes we had lost many links with the fighting battalions. I heard no more from the 4th/5th Black Watch until I heard that it had been almost smashed out of existence. Its strength at the end of the German sweep towards Amiens was one officer and thirty other ranks, and the whole Brigade became a single unit. But we did not know until after the War how the battalion had been massacred. The survivors

said there was no panic. All fought grimly
till they were knocked out, with R.S.M. Hutton
an inspiration to all ranks. He, at least, of all my
comrades, ought to have had the V.C.

The general impression at midsummer was that
the Germans would be beaten by the spring, and
we all expected to be in at the finish. Captain
Lawrence thought the Germans would stand on
the Hindenburg line and hold out till 1920.
Physically I was now in good form, but became a
slight casualty in August. I was playing Rugby,
and when on the ground was kicked above the
left eye by an officer-instructor. As he had had
an arm blown off he had to use his feet for tackling.
He did so vigorously, and I was a wounded warrior
with a white bandage over the left brow for some
time. The scar just above the eye remained for
several years, and people never believed me when
I told them I received this injury at football. They
thought this was my variation of the joke of the
weary, bandaged soldier who, on being asked for
the thousandth time whether he was wounded by
the Germans, replied to the old lady : " No, mum,
I was kicked by the canary."

As good news came from the Front we relaxed
and enjoyed life, but we were eager to pass our
final examinations. At the Front it had seemed
easy, if you had the right education and a little
experience of fighting, to get a commission, but it
seemed now a very difficult honour to attain. That
was a good sign. Clearly we were not short of
officers, and there were other signs that we were
not short of men. For example, my landlady's

two sons were sent home for the harvest, the golden abundance of which that year was a joy to the eye. Those marshalled stooks, tied with straw bands, of locally-varying paterns, as by some regimental custom, spelt war strength to the dullest mind.

We felt certain that 1919 would finish the War, but our instructors spoke scornfully of optimistic newspaper drivel. As the examination neared I became more and more afraid of failing. I felt it would mar my career for life if I, mentor of generals and critic of Cabinets, were not considered good enough to be a second-lieutenant. I felt that the War had taken the edge off such mental powers as God gave me.

We sat our final on 24th September, hesitant and gloomy at first, but reassured as the day went on. We were given four days' rest after it; a rest, not leave. That is, we got no ration allowance and no permission to travel by rail, but could go where we liked by bicycle. My wife and I went off to Tarbet and Loch Lomond, I cycling through heavy weather and being much concerned because a new trench-coat, for which I had paid five pounds ten shillings, got wet through. I shall never forget Loch Lomond, sombre in mist that drifted, smoke-like, about the craggy heights, for it was there that we first read newspapers that spoke of the beginning of the end.

When we returned there was no word of examination results, and rumour-mongering was rife. My contribution was to suggest that everybody had passed but that secrecy was to be maintained till

the end of the course for disciplinary purposes. I
think this was true. I was told I was first in tactics
and field engineering, but, curiously enough, I did
not do so well in military law, a subject upon which
I had once been an orderly-room authority.

CHAPTER XLII

THE BEGINNING OF THE END

IT was dazzlingly exciting to think that the tremendous result was at hand, a smashed and humbled Germany. I wrote in my diary on 13th October: " I see Britain to-day as a vista of little homes where women hardly know what to do to contain themselves—of men seeking newspapers that were sold out hours ago—of vindictive little civilian groups talking of a fit end for the Kaiser—of soldiers wondering what luck they will have in the labour market. I do not think there will be much celebrating. We only know one way of celebrating in this country (Scotland), and whisky is almost unobtainable. It do not feel wholly jubilant myself. I have long felt we shall go back to a shadowed, embittered and burdened life of struggle."

19th October: " After the confusion and excitements on receipt of the German Armistice proposals the situation has cleared within limits. An ugly, grasping spirit is powerful in this country, a determined greed for great indemnities, a belief that, though Germany failed to make War pay, we may succeed. This is the feeling of what I may call the War interests, and is dreaded—yes, *dreaded*, by the poor creatures whose sons are fighting, and who pray for peace. My landlady says, with a queer, hurt surprise, like a child suddenly confronted with the evil in life : ' There are people who don't want the War to stop.' "

We were kept hard at it till the end. A new company of cadets arrived at Gailes on 18th October. I had the honour of making a speech of welcome on behalf of the senior company. The new-comers listened appreciatively, and under their applause I became fluent and sentimental. Once or twice I offered to stop but they cried, " Go on!" It was the audience of my life. Little did these greenhorns guess that the speech was to keep them in the dining-room while a raiding party did its dirty work in their huts. Had we not suffered in just the same way?

Peace talk quietened down in October, and the word of the day was "Fight on". Mr. Churchill became suspect by the Jingoes for pleading that the German people should not be trampled to the dust. Then with November came the shooting of Tisza by his soldiers, Hungary, Bulgaria, Bohemia and German-Austria declared republics, and the Kaiser's flight to his Army headquarters.

Then, to the surprise of many of the cadets, who disbelieved the Press, came the end. About 11 o'clock on the great day, as we were changing into slacks and jerseys for physical training, a cheer broke out down at the end of the camp, near the post-office hut. The cheer spread by an infection of jocularity, but it was no false start. A big Union Jack went up over the orderly-room, and soon the bolder men were shouting, " We—want—a—holiday."

A march round the camp began, pipers playing, signal-flags waving, men singing. Soon eightsome reels were going on, and the W.A.A.C.s came out and marched and danced, too. It was hopeless to expect parades to go on. It was announced that there would be a holiday after a service at 2 p.m.

The canteen was opened and the men found plenty to celebrate with. We were too excited to eat when we went into lunch, but pelted each other with potatoes, kissed the waitresses again and again, and sang the old soldier-songs. I slipped off to my little cottage, where already flags were waving in the golden sunshine. My wife, who had been brave and cheerful in every crisis, now gave way, for the first time, to tears—tears of joy.

Celebrations in the camp soon subsided. After the first brief outburst there was less excitement than over a big football match. Parades went on as usual. The cadets were in no hurry to leave the comfortable shelter of the Army. We had grown used to its ways in four and a half years, and looked forward anxiously to the civilian scramble to live. It was a great grievance with us that the munition workers were at once freed to get what jobs were now going, whilst we were kept in the Army.

We were warned officially that we might be required to officer troops to proceed against Russia. I wrote on 1st December: " One feels a little suspicious of the Army authorities. They seem in no hurry to give up their power over the millions of soldiers who have not the slightest intention of serving again once they get out of khaki. Thousands of officers have had the time of their lives and are sorry it is nearing an end."

We were allowed home for Christmas, and I went diffidently into the office of the *Daily Mail* to ask for work. I found an old Aberdonian, C. I. Beattie, acting as editor. Both he and, later, Lord Northcliffe gave me the friendliest of welcomes, and I was given the chance I wanted. Lord Northcliffe asked me much about Army life. He wanted to know, too, what school I was at, and when I told him I was a Christ's Hospital boy he said he had never known a boy from that school fail to do well. Many journalists have spoken of him as a ruthless Napoleon of Fleet Street. I found him a warm-hearted encourager.

The great moment of release from the Army came on 8th January, 1919, and I was demobilized at the Crystal Palace with the rank of second-lieutenant, unpaid. So I became an officer after all.

CHAPTER XLIII

THANKSGIVING

NOW that I come to the end of my story I wonder whether I have brought home as I meant to do the spirit of my old battalion, once so gay, then shattered and re-made again and again, but going on staunchly to the end?

I shall not forget to my dying day the trials we went through; aching backs, aching feet, aching eyes, aching heads, and, worst of all, aching hearts; dragging marches, nightmare carrying-parties, standing in water, the nerve-racking sensations of being bombed by an aeroplane flying low over our camp, the hopelessness that settled upon our spirits as the casualties grew, the agony of long fighting spells in the line, and yet, amid the worst of it all, courage and good-fellowship.

We were doomed to tread with bleeding feet an unimaginable *via dolorosa* before we came to the Day of Peace. The Peace Treaty proved no triumph of state-craft. It created fresh scope for dissension. We find, even now, there is very little of the pride of success among the victor nations, and the victim nations still burn with resentment. In this country of ours the one widespread and heart-felt celebration of the War is our commemoration of the dead. Our orators do not proclaim that the War was a boon for which to thank God. They do not even seek to convince us that we gained credit by it, and theirs is the right attitude, for if anyone began to say that it was a great landmark of world progress we should begin to think how, for four years, it crucified a great part of mankind, and we should be confronted with the almost intolerable thought of the twenty million soldiers, sailors and civilians who perished in it.

I believe that we can say truthfully, in the presence of the dead who compass us about and are so affectionately remembered, that they fought in an honourable cause. They longed to be remembered. When those brave boys of ours fixed bayonets to advance, each would give his chum some farewell message to those at home, just in case . . . Oftener than not that message was a roughly tender plea for remembrance. When a man lay dying in the trench he would say to his own familiar friend : " You'll tell the girl I played the game, won't you? Tell her not to forget me." And when, after many months of suffering and disappointment, the end of the War seemed to recede, and a man fighting in the line thought little of his chance of a safe return, our boys longed with passionate anxiety that their country, for which they must die, would not blot them out of its thoughts when peace came.

The home-coming was never the triumph our men expected. Battalions were destroyed again and again, and their remains merged into new units with the remnants of others. What to many was "the old Batt." did not march back through the town it had left. The triumphal marches in London were not all we had hoped for. Many of those standing with wet eyes, and sometimes in ragged clothes, in the crowd that watched had seen far more fighting than the boyish recruits who now marched with such precision. But there was no room in an old soldier's heart for envy. We were compassed about, when the London streets were solemn with military pageantry, by the innumerable company of our dead. They, too, came to the tuck of the drum. They come each year now on that sacred day, when, thinking of the War, we think most of the end of those brave young lives.

We almost forget for a moment that they are the blessed dead. They are living and laughing boys again. Dear, great-hearted comrades of the Black Watch, no darkness of the grave can keep you from my sight, nothing can dim the light of youth in your friendly eyes. You will never be old ghosts to me, but warm-hearted friends, as when we stood in the line together and talked of our dear ones at home.

The horrors of those years have often haunted my dreams, but I thank God with a humble heart that I came to know and love the spirit of my old battalion.

THE END